Exploring the Basic Income Guarantee

Series Editor
Karl Widerquist
Georgetown University in Qatar
Doha, Qatar

Basic income is one of the most innovative, powerful, straightforward, and controversial proposals for addressing poverty and growing inequalities. A Basic Income Guarantee (BIG) is designed to be an unconditional, government-insured guarantee that all citizens will have enough income to meet their basic needs. The concept of basic, or guaranteed, income is a form of social provision and this series examines the arguments for and against it from an interdisciplinary perspective with special focus on the economic and social factors. By systematically connecting abstract philosophical debates over competing principles of BIG to the empirical analysis of concrete policy proposals, this series contributes to the fields of economics, politics, social policy, and philosophy and establishes a theoretical framework for interdisciplinary research. It will bring together international and national scholars and activists to provide a comparative look at the main efforts to date to pass unconditional BIG legislation across regions of the globe and will identify commonalities and differences across countries drawing lessons for advancing social policies in general and BIG policies in particular.

More information about this series at
http://www.palgrave.com/gp/series/14981

Leah Hamilton

Welfare Doesn't Work

The Promises of Basic Income for a Failed American Safety Net

palgrave
macmillan

Leah Hamilton
Department of Social Work
Appalachian State University
Boone, NC, USA

ISSN 2662-3803 ISSN 2662-3811 (electronic)
Exploring the Basic Income Guarantee
ISBN 978-3-030-37120-3 ISBN 978-3-030-37121-0 (eBook)
https://doi.org/10.1007/978-3-030-37121-0

This Palgrave Pivot imprint is published by the registered company Springer Nature Switzerland AG.
The registered company address is: Gewerbestrasse 11, 6330 Cham, Switzerland

To G and F; I wrote these words while you slept in my arms, hoping that your mama could make your future world just a tiny bit better.

And to J; the man who reminds me that I take on too much but supports me when I do it anyway.

Contents

Abbreviations

AACWA	Adoption Assistance and Child Welfare Act of 1980
AFDC	Aid to Families with Dependent Children
ASFA	Adoption and Safe Families Act of 1997
BIEN	Basic Income Earth Network
CAPTA	Child Abuse Prevention and Treatment Act of 1974
EITC	Earned Income Tax Credit
LIHEAP	Low Income Home Energy Assistance Program
LPR	Labor Force Participation Rate
NIT	Negative Income Tax
PRWORA	Personal Responsibility and Work Opportunity Reconciliation Act of 1996
SNAP	Supplemental Nutrition Assistance Program
SSI	Supplemental Security Income
TANF	Temporary Assistance for Needy Families
UBI	Universal Basic Income
USBIG	US Basic Income Guarantee

Introduction[1]

Democrats and Republicans don't see eye to eye often, but they can safely agree on one point: Welfare doesn't work. Liberals are concerned that an ever-shrinking social safety net reaches fewer and fewer families in need, and Republicans worry that welfare benefits create dependence. They are both right.

The primary welfare program in the United States, Temporary Assistance to Needy Families, served 68% of low-income families in 1996. As of 2017, only 23% of low-income families received assistance (Floyd, Pavetti, & Schott, 2015). This change has been largely brought about by the imposition of five-year lifetime limits (states are allowed to set lower limits) and stricter eligibility criteria. Reductions in cash assistance have been solidly linked to the rise of deep poverty in America (H. L. Shaefer & Edin, 2018), family strain, and increased foster care placements (Swann & Sylvester, 2006). Nearly 1.5 million US households (including 2.8 million children) lived on less than $2 per person per day in 2011 (Shaefer & Edin, 2012) (the World Bank's measurement of extreme poverty).

Meanwhile, welfare eligibility rules designed to encourage independence have achieved the opposite effect. For example, though many states impose strict work requirements, states that loosen these rules see recipients move to a higher wage, higher benefit work (Lim, Coulton, & Lalich, 2009), presumably because they have the breathing room to search for a good job rather than take the first one that comes along. Similarly, in states

[1] Previously appeared in https://basicincome.org/news/2018/06/why-welfare-doesnt-work-and-what-we-should-do-instead/

with strict limitations on recipient assets, low-income families are less likely to own a car (Hamilton, 2017), making it nearly impossible to maintain employment in areas without public transportation. Even worse, some researchers are discovering a "cliff effect" in which welfare recipients immediately lose all benefits (including child care assistance) after a small increase in income (Ahn, 2014; Roll & East, 2014). As a result, many parents turn down promotional opportunities because they would be ultimately worse off financially. Any parent would make the same decision if it meant the ability to feed their children and afford quality childcare.

We must redesign this entire system. While we boast the highest GDP in the world (World Bank, 2017), it is ludicrous that children are growing up in the kind of deprivation we usually associate with developing countries. Simultaneously, we must ensure that no one is discouraged from growing their income or assets. One potential solution is a universal basic income (UBI), which provides an annual benefit to every citizen. With this one simple policy, we can achieve many goals of both the left and right. Poverty is eliminated overnight, work disincentives are removed, and American bureaucracy is significantly reduced. Families are then free to make financial decisions without government intrusion. And in the long run, we save money. Childhood poverty alone costs the US $1.03 trillion (Schoenherr, 2018) (yes, trillion) per year. In the twenty-first century, eradicating poverty isn't complicated. We're just going about it in the worst possible way.

After five years as a front-line foster care social worker, I became convinced that families were set up to fail under current social policy. I watched too many families separated and children placed in long-term foster care; not because their parents were fundamentally bad people, but because we lack some of the fundamental supports seen in other countries. I returned to graduate school and eventually received a Ph.D. in Public Policy. I now teach future social workers and conduct research on welfare policy and family economic success. This book will explore the incentives and effects of current welfare policy, contrasted with outcomes for the various basic income pilots throughout the world over the past 70 years. Case examples from my own work with families in the foster care system, interviews with basic income pilot recipients in Ontario, Canada, and a survey of 50 American Amazon Mechanical Turk Workers (also known as MTurkers) who have received public assistance will be woven throughout the book to better illustrate the effects of our current system and the hidden potential of more radical alternatives.

References

Ahn, H. (2014). Economic Well-Being of Low-Income Single-Mother Families Following Welfare Reform in the USA. *International Journal of Social Welfare, 24*(1), 14–26. https://doi.org/10.1111/ijsw.12095.

Floyd, I., Pavetti, L., & Schott, L. (2015). *TANF Reaching Few Poor Families.* Retrieved from Center for Budget Policies and Priorities Website: https://www.cbpp.org/research/family-income-support/tanf-reaching-few-poor-families

Hamilton, L. (2017). *Asset Limits in Public Assistance and Savings Behavior Among Low-Income Families.* Retrieved from Pew Charitable Trusts Website: http://www.pewtrusts.org/~/media/assets/2017/09/asset_limits_in_public_assistance_and_savings_behavior_among_low_income_families.pdf

Lim, Y., Coulton, C., & Lalich, N. (2009). State TANF Policies and Employment Outcomes Among Welfare Leavers. *Social Service Review, 84*(4), 525–555.

Roll, S., & East, J. (2014). Financially Vulnerable Families and the Child Care Cliff Effect. *Journal of Poverty, 18*(2), 169–187. https://doi.org/10.1080/10875549.2014.896307.

Schoenherr, N. (2018, April 16). Childhood Poverty Costs U.S. $1.03 Trillion in a Year, Study Finds. Retrieved October 24, 2018, from The Source Website: https://source.wustl.edu/2018/04/childhood-poverty-cost-u-s-1-03-trillion-in-a-year-study-finds/

Shaefer, H. L., & Edin, K. (2018). *Welfare Reform and the Families It Left Behind* (pp. 22–27). Retrieved from Stanford Center on Poverty & Inequality Website: https://inequality.stanford.edu/sites/default/files/Pathways_Winter2018_Families-Left-Behind.pdf

Shaefer, L., & Edin, K. (2012). *Extreme Poverty in the United States, 1996 to 2011* (Policy Brief No. 5; p. 5). Retrieved from National Poverty Center Website: http://npc.umich.edu/publications/policy_briefs/brief28/policybrief28.pdf

Swann, C. A., & Sylvester, M. S. (2006). The Foster Care Crisis: What Caused Caseloads to Grow? *Demography, 43*(2), 309–335.

World Bank. (2017). *Gross Domestic Product.* Retrieved from https://databank.worldbank.org/data/download/GDP.pdf

CHAPTER 1

A Tale of Two Ideas

Abstract Since the fall of feudalism in Europe, western governments have implemented minimal and punitive public assistance programs to maintain a delicate balance between preventing revolt and ensuring a steady stream of workers willing to accept meager wages. While advocates throughout history have presented an alternative, the universal basic income (UBI), the inexhaustible need for cheap labor created by agriculture and industrialization has proven an infertile ground for UBI ideals. Rising inequality and automation of the twentieth and twenty-first centuries, however, have created renewed interest in basic income, which may present the solution to ineffective modern welfare policy.

Keywords Welfare • Race • Revolution • Basic income

My first job out of college was as a caseworker for children in foster care with developmental disabilities. I was responsible for ensuring that my clients received appropriate educational accommodations at school and that their foster parents were providing the level of specialized care they required. One 17-year-old boy (I'll call him "Thomas") had a severe form of cerebral palsy. He used a wheelchair, had significant intellectual delays, did not speak, or even swallow. His foster parents fed him through a g-tube, which is a port on the outside of the body connected directly to

L. Hamilton, *Welfare Doesn't Work*, Exploring the Basic Income Guarantee, https://doi.org/10.1007/978-3-030-37121-0_1

the stomach. Unable to dress, bath, or feed himself, Thomas required around-the-clock support from a full-time caretaker. He was one of five children born to a dedicated, but low-income, single mother (whom I'll call "Sue"). Because Thomas' needs were so demanding, making it nearly impossible to hold down a job, Sue essentially had two choices before her. She could raise five children on Thomas' $750 per month in disability payments and maybe a few hundred more in Food Stamps and Housing Assistance, or she could surrender Thomas to foster care.

When Thomas was inevitably placed in care, his foster parents were granted a significantly higher reimbursement rate than most foster children due to his high level of needs, $3000 per month. I never met his mother, but I can only imagine the guilt a parent would feel at having to make such a decision and maybe also frustration at the inequity of it. Over time, Sue visited Thomas less and less, likely as her way to cope and move on from this impossible situation. As a young social worker, this case was my first clue that something was deeply wrong with our social welfare system. This family was divided, not because it saved taxpayer money, but because modern American social policy is constructed with a suspicious eye toward people in poverty, lest a child like Thomas and his mother seek to "game" the system.

While the American welfare system seems to have reached new heights of political polarization, mistrust of the poor has been a defining characteristic of social assistance and public relief programs for hundreds of years. Rather than providing a "safety net," Frances Fox Piven and Richard Cloward first described the history of welfare in the Western world as a balancing act between maintaining social order and ensuring a steady stream of cheap labor for industry (Piven & Cloward, 1993). This balance has traditionally been accomplished by expanding the social safety net in times of economic decline and contracting it once again as the economy recovers so that workers are compelled to accept any wages offered. We will return to the relationship between welfare and labor in Chap. 2.

In this chapter, we will focus on the ways that economic change influences social unrest and how leaders have historically responded. At every turn, leaders maintain this balancing act by offering just enough assistance to prevent outright revolution while pushing a narrative that those unwilling or unable to accept dangerous or exploitative employment conditions are sinful, lazy, or both. Alongside this history, a few advocates have proposed that instead of trying to appease the proletariat, we treat all citizens as equally deserving of having their basic needs met, regardless of circumstance, through a regular, unconditional assistance payment, known today as a universal basic income (UBI).

A *Very* Brief History of Welfare in Early Europe

The fall of feudalism in Europe created rapid social change. Former serfs were displaced and, as is always the case during times of economic upheaval, were not immediately absorbed into some new occupation. Further declining death rates contributed to a population boom, and with insufficient jobs to absorb the sudden increase in workers, many found themselves in abject poverty. Local governments across Europe attempted to control the growing problem of vagrancy with penalties for begging. When simply punishing the poor was insufficient to control the tumult, communities began establishing the double-edged systems of public relief and tight social control, as those in poverty were believed to be prone to idleness and immorality. Lyon, France, for example, instituted cash assistance, but church rectors followed recipients to ensure that benefits were not spent on alcohol or gambling. In England, local authorities registered the poor and provided them with documents which were essentially a license to beg. If anyone was found to be begging without this documentation, they were subject to a public whipping (Piven & Cloward, 1993).

During the European Renaissance, charitable functions slowly began moving from church to state responsibility (in England, it may not be coincidental that much of this movement occurred during the reign of Henry VIII and Elizabeth I, both of whom—for their own reasons—sought to reduce the power of the Catholic church). To more systematically and humanely address the problem of pauperism, the prominent theologists Sir Thomas More, Lord Chancellor under Henry VIII, and Johannes Ludovicus Vives urged governments to provide every citizen with a minimum income, arguing that "no one should die of hunger" (Vives, 2002). More's *Utopia*, first published in 1516, is believed by many to be the first introduction of basic income ideas (Standing, 2017).

> I once happened to be dining with the Cardinal when a certain English lawyer was there. I forgot how the subject came up, but he was speaking with great enthusiasm about the stern measures that were then being taken against thieves. 'We're hanging them all over the place', he said. 'I've seen

> as many as twenty on a single gallows. And that's what I find so odd. Considering how few of them get away with it, how come we are still plagued with so many robbers?' 'What's odd about it?', I asked—for I never hesitated to speak freely in front of the Cardinal. This method of dealing with thieves is both unjust and undesirable. As a punishment, it's too severe, and as a deterrent, it's quite ineffective. Petty larceny isn't bad enough to deserve the death penalty. And no penalty on earth will stop people from stealing, if it's their only way of getting food. In this respect, you English, like most other nations, remind me of these incompetent schoolmasters, who prefer caning their pupils to teaching them. Instead of inflicting these horrible punishments, it would be far more to the point to provide everyone with some means of livelihood, so that nobody's under the frightful necessity of becoming, first a thief, and then a corpse. (More, 2003)

However, More and Vives also believed that the poor must be willing to work and prove themselves deserving of aid. This latter notion was adopted wholeheartedly into the Elizabethan Poor Laws of 1601, which separated the poor into categories of "deserving" and "undeserving," or those who cannot work (e.g., the elderly and disabled) and those who presumably could, but do not work. The Poor Laws provided "outdoor" relief (assistance in the recipient's own home) for the "deserving," which included food, clothing, and other essential materials. The "undeserving" were placed in poorhouses and indentured servitude, otherwise known as "indoor relief." Orphans and the children of the poor were placed in apprenticeships to teach them the "Christian" value of hard work and to prevent them from inheriting their parent's "idleness" (Jansson, 2014).

It must be noted, of course, that the English elite did not believe that idleness was sinful for *them*, as most looked down upon any labor among the nobility. But the system of a leisure class required an enormous underclass available to work around the clock (long before the establishment of labor laws) as servants, farmers, and manual laborers. It also required an unlimited supply of soldiers available to die in the frequent skirmishes between European monarchs (Isenberg, 2017). Therefore, it would never do for those born into poverty to believe they had any right to basic security outside of hard work for meager wages.

This balance of scant assistance and social control was more or less maintained until the late 1700s when revolutionary ideas fermented in France and threatened to upend the entire European monarchical economy. An early leader of the French Revolution, the Marquis de Condorcet, proposed free education, gender, and racial equality, and a scheme akin to a basic income (Basic Income Earth Network, 2018). Though he was imprisoned before his ideas could be fully implemented, the French Revolution put fear in the hearts of the powerful across Europe. The English elite worked quickly to prevent such an upheaval in their own country by increasing public relief six times between 1760 and 1818 (Piven & Cloward, 1993).

American Bootstraps

The English spirit of punishment for those believed to be capable but unwilling to work intertwined seamlessly within the Protestant work ethic of early American settlers. Recipients of welfare in the early colonies were required to wear the letter "P" for pauper, could be imprisoned, sold into indentured servitude or slavery, or blocked form marrying (Joseph, 2006). As Americans explored their new land with seemingly endless natural resources, the philosopher Thomas Paine believed that every adult American had a natural birthright to the land and should, therefore, be paid an annual "ground-rent," funded by taxes on agriculture (Basic Income Earth Network, 2018). But these ideas were preposterous to most in the era of slavery and indentured servitude. Westward expansion and settlement brought with it an inexhaustible need for hard—often deadly—labor and only further reinforced the high cultural value placed on work and independence, with slothfulness seen as sinful.

Further, because early American settlers were escaping corrupt and all-powerful monarchies in Europe, they framed the Constitution to decentralize power and placed many functions, including poor relief, in the hands of state and local government. They also believed there would be little need for significant intervention, as their new utopian society would be free from the social ills that plagued Europe (Jansson, 2014). Article 1, Section 8 of the Constitution states that "The Congress shall have the Power to lay and collect Taxes, Duties, Imposts, and Excises, to pay the Debts and provide for the common defense and general welfare of the United States," but this has historically been defined narrowly. Over time, the "general welfare clause"—as it is more commonly known—has been interpreted more broadly by the courts (including the upholding of the Social Security Act by the Supreme Court in 1937) (Abramovitz, 1996), but remains controversial to this day (Jansson, 2014). For example, during the economic depressions of 1893, 1914, and 1921, there were efforts in Congress to provide national relief for the unemployed, but each was defeated, with opponents arguing that relief was, constitutionally, a local and not federal responsibility.

The era of industrialization, however, altered human life in ways unpredictable to the Founding Fathers. Millions moved from small farming communities to manufacturing opportunities in large cities. Meanwhile, poor, European immigrants found their way to American shores, including 1.2 million Irish escaping the potato famine of 1845–1849 (Jansson, 2014). Cities lacked the housing, employment, sanitation, and relief infrastructure to respond to the growing need adequately. As a result, concentrated poverty overwhelmed America's urban centers. Crime and civil unrest threatened to boil over. Bertrand Russell and other writers called again for the establishment of a basic income, arguing that "when education is finished, no one should be compelled to work, and those who choose not to work should receive a bare livelihood, and be left completely free" (Russell, 2013). Here too, these ideas held little sway in an industrializing America with a nearly endless need for cheap and expendable labor. Factory work was difficult and dangerous, producing many casualties. Progressive Era advocates were successful, however, in establishing Mother's Pensions, the first federal welfare program, as a necessary support for women who were widowed by dangerous working conditions and to prevent the placement of their children in costly orphanages.

Just as in old Europe, the American government was able to maintain sufficient social order by providing minimal support to the most deserving during this time of rapid economic expansion. But like the fall of feudalism and the French Revolution before it, the Crash of 1929 and subsequent Great Depression threatened the delicate balance of society. Employment fell by 40% and wages fell by a third between 1929 and 1932. Families fell rapidly into extreme poverty, and childhood malnutrition increased significantly (Abramovitz, 1996). Simultaneously, droughts in American farmlands, graphically depicted in John Steinbeck's *The Grapes of Wrath*, dislocated countless sharecroppers. From 1929 to 1932, annual American agricultural income fell from $7 billion to $2 billion dollars (Piven & Cloward, 1993).

President Herbert Hoover resisted committing the federal government to relief efforts for the unemployed; instead, sending financial support to businesses and justifying declining wages as necessary to ensure continued profits for the American economy. Relief for the unemployed instead fell upon local governments, which were overwhelmed by the sudden need.

The situation became unstable. Unemployed workers began inundating relief offices, sometimes conducting sit-ins until relief was granted. As a result, the monthly average of 33,861 households receiving local aid in 1929 increased to 1,287,778 in 1931 (Piven & Cloward, 1993). Still, as the Depression worsened and no assistance from the federal government was provided, demonstrations and marches occurred frequently. Mobs of the unemployed gathered to move the furniture of evicted families back into their apartments, even if the family was not there.

The establishment of American Democracy means that workers no longer need to revolt to register their discontent. They can simply walk into a voting booth. Capitalists and political leaders of the 1930s recognized the danger posed by millions of unemployed and dissatisfied voters, instituting "pauper exclusion laws," which removed voting rights from those receiving public aid (Stiglitz, 2012). Thankfully, these laws were insufficient to completely disenfranchise the poor, who demanded more significant federal intervention to end the Depression. In the election of 1932, Herbert Hoover was defeated by Franklin Delano Roosevelt, who proposed a work relief program (the Civilian Conservation Corps) and assistance to the unemployed within three weeks of assuming office. Federal aid expanded to one in six households by the end of 1934, and average monthly household grants rose from $15.15 in 1933 to $29.33 in 1935 (Piven & Cloward, 1993).

Still, some felt that Roosevelt had not gone far enough. Senator Huey Long's "Share Our Wealth" movement, popular among the southern working class, advocated for an annual guaranteed income of $5000 per household (Standing, 2017). Had he not been assassinated in 1935, Senator Long was seen as a viable contender for the Democratic nomination in the 1936 presidential election, capturing 10% of the vote in a national poll (Abramovitz, 1996). While this might not have been sufficient to win the presidency, his movement threatened to split the Democratic party. Partially as an attempt to bring working-class Democrats back into the fold, Roosevelt proposed the Social Security Act of 1935, which established the Social Security and Unemployment Insurance programs as we know them today. The Social Security Act also created the first federal disability support program, Aid to the Blind, and transformed Mothers Pensions programs into Aid to Dependent Children (later Aid to Families with Dependent Children or AFDC).

Essentially, the Social Security Act provided federal relief to the elderly, children, workers who were temporarily unemployed, and the blind, but opponents were certain that it signaled the rise of Communism in America. Roosevelt appeased these critics by dismantling most other federal relief to working aged males and conjuring the age-old descriptions of those unwilling to accept any employment condition as sinful. In his annual message to Congress in January 1935, he said that "Continued dependence upon relief induces a spiritual and moral disintegration fundamentally destructive to the national fiber" (Roosevelt, 1935).

The Civil Rights Movement

The next threat to the balance of social order came in the 1960s and '70s when the Women's and Civil Rights movements pushed for an expanded welfare state. On Mother's Day, 1968, Coretta Scott King led a march of 5000 welfare recipients in Washington, D.C., demanding the end of unjust and racist welfare laws. As a response to these movements, welfare rolls increased by 107% over the decade, compared to just 17% in the booming post-war economy of the 1950s (Piven & Cloward, 1993). The Great Society era also saw the establishment of many of the social safety programs we rely on today, including Head Start, Medicare, Medicaid, and Food Stamps.

Meanwhile, more radical proposals of a basic income were pushed by an unlikely cadre including Martin Luther King Jr., conservative economists, President Johnson, and even President Nixon. In 1962, Milton Friedman, a leader of the Chicago School of Economics, which views the market as self-correcting and in need of minimal government intervention, proposed a negative income tax, which is essentially a refundable tax credit to every citizen under a certain income threshold. Friedman saw this as more straightforward and effective than the patchwork of American social welfare programs (Friedman, 2009). From a more social justice focused perspective, Dr. King wrote, "I am now convinced that the simplest approach will prove to be the most effective—the solution to poverty is to abolish it directly by a now widely discussed measure: the guaranteed income…The dignity of the individual will flourish when the decisions concerning his life are in his own hands" (King, 2010).

Due to rapid social change in the 1960s and through the work of such diverse advocates, for the first time in history, a basic income seemed to many as having "such unassailable logic that it would shortly be the law of the land" (Bell & Bushe, 1975, p. 176). Several basic income and negative tax pilots launched during this era. Between 1968 and 1972, in New

Jersey and Scranton, Pennsylvania, 1300 low-income families were recruited and then randomly assigned to "treatment" and "control" groups in an experiment sponsored by the federal Office of Economic Opportunity (OEO). Control group families were tracked but did not receive a basic income. Treatment families were then further divided into those receiving 50, 75, 100, and 125% of the official poverty line—$1650, $2475, $3300, and $4125 annually for a family of four—in basic income payments. Treatment and control families both completed regular questionnaires regarding their "participation in the labor force, financial status, medical and educational history, family structure, and political and social integration" (Katz, 1973, p. 111).

The OEO also launched a pilot in rural counties of Iowa and North Carolina between 1970 and 1972 with 810 families. Similar to the New Jersey and Pennsylvania experiment, OEO divided families into treatment and control groups, with treatment groups receiving either 50, 75, or 100% of the poverty line. In addition to workforce involvement, health, family stability, finances, and civic engagement, the rural study tracked nutrition, the school performance of children, and whether basic income influenced the rate at which families moved from rural to urban areas.

Interestingly, a second federal department, the U.S. Department of Health, Education, and Welfare funded its pilots in Seattle, Washington, and Denver, Colorado, from 1970 to 1978 and Gary, Indiana from 1971 to 1974. The Seattle/Denver Income Maintenance Experiment, also known as SIME/DIME, included 5202 families with 60% of those receiving a basic income and 40% comprising a control group. Like the other pilots, the treatment families received a range of benefits. Participants all had low incomes, with 20% being former recipients of AFDC. These experiments measured effects to workforce participation, "family stability, parent child interactions, the effects of race on poverty, a comparison of sociocultural differences in various cities, and the relationship of family stability to participation in the labor market" (Katz, 1973, p. 113). The Gary, Indiana experiment with 1684 families was designed similarly to the other pilots, except that a significant proportion of recipients were single, black mothers, and the researchers attempted to capture whether basic income influenced the rate at which participants accessed other social services.

A more ambitious pilot was launched in Canada which offered basic income to the entire town of Dauphin, Manitoba—approximately 10,000 residents—between 1974 and 1979 (Marinescu, 2017). This type of experiment is called “saturation,” in which you can observe effects to the entire community when everyone is receiving a basic income. This strategy has significant advantages over smaller experiments. For example, while an experimental project can tell you whether the treatment group was more or less likely to continue working in comparison to the control group, a saturation project can tell you whether there were any effects to the overall employment rate. This distinction is important because one could hypothetically argue that in the former instance, a person who worked more hours was actually taking a job from someone else, with a net zero effect to the employment rate. Unfortunately, data collection discontinued after the first two years of the Dauphin pilot and analysis was never conducted until Dr. Evelyn Forget, an Economist at the University of Manitoba, and her colleagues recovered the archived records in 2011.

In 1976, Alaskan voters established the Alaska Permanent Fund, which creates an annual dividend for every citizen, including children, from the state’s oil revenue. The value of the dividend fluctuates—depending on revenues—and has ranged from $331 in 1984 to $2072 in 2015 (Marinescu, 2017). While not intended as a UBI experiment, the Alaska Permanent Fund has given researchers a great deal of insight into the effects of a statewide, unconditional, universal income payment. There will be greater discussion about each of these experiments in future chapters.

Amid growing interest in basic income, President Nixon advocated in 1972 for the Family Assistance Plan, which was similar to a negative income tax (Standing, 2017), and proposed a minimum annual income of $500 each for the first two members of the household and $300 for each additional member (equivalent to $9811 for a family of four in 2018 dollars) (Piven & Cloward, 1993). But unlike a true basic income, the plan did not cover people who do not work at all. It was defeated in Congress by Democrats and advocates such as the National Welfare Rights Organization and even Milton Friedman who believed that the plan was insufficient (Withorn, 2006). However, basic income’s political momentum influenced Congress to transform the original Aid to the Blind program into the more extensive Supplemental Security Income (SSI) program for all people with disabilities (Social Security Administration, 2018).

Race and Welfare

No discussion of welfare in the United States is complete without understanding the influence of American racial politics. While the specific effects of welfare policy on women and children will be delineated in future chapters, racism and racial inequality are so central to American welfare policy that they must be woven throughout our discussion. Federal relief programs were designed very early to ensure that white mothers and widows were the primary beneficiaries. In the 1920s and '30s, many localities with high African American populations simply lacked Mother's Pension offices (Gooden & Douglas, 2006). When African American mothers did receive aid, it was frequently much less than their white counterparts. Some offices had two separate sample budgets, one for white families and one for black families, based upon the assumption that the later could survive on less (Green, 2015).

As the Civil Rights movement addressed many of the overtly racist elements of welfare policy and the program expanded to black families, public support for the program declined (Gooden & Douglas, 2006). A great deal of research suggests that race continues to underscore modern welfare policy. For example, states with higher proportions of African Americans implement more paternalistic and punitive eligibility rules (Soss, Fording, & Schram, 2008). These states are more likely to impose strict time limits, punitive sanction policies, family caps (denying assistance when additional children are born), and denial of benefits to applicants who have a felony conviction. They also tend to have lower income eligibility guidelines (meaning that you have to make less to qualify) and lower monthly benefits (Hahn, Aron, Lou, Pratt, & Okoli, 2017).

The Conservative Revolution

White backlash to the Civil Rights movement of the 1960s had significant repercussions for the American welfare system. Presidential candidate Ronald Reagan capitalized on a growing fear among white voters by speaking on the campaign trail of a "welfare queen" who "used 80 names, 30 addresses, 15 telephone numbers to collect Food Stamps, Social Security, veterans' benefits for four nonexistent deceased veteran husbands, as well as welfare. Her tax-free cash income alone has been running $150,000 a year" (Levin, 2013). The woman he was referring to, Linda Taylor, was also suspected of fraud, kidnapping, and even murder (Levin,

2019), but these details were never mentioned as they would have distracted from Reagan's intended effect: to paint her as symptomatic of a lax welfare state, rather than as a criminal outlier. As President, Reagan moved quickly to fulfill his promises, removing 491,000 people with disabilities from the SSI program (Piven & Cloward, 1993) and 400,000 families from the AFDC program (Abramovitz, 1996) in the first years of his administration.

The primary cash assistance program in the United States, AFDC, faced considerable scrutiny in this new political climate. The inflation-adjusted value of welfare benefits fell 42% between 1970 and 1990 (Piven & Cloward, 1993). In 1996, amid growing conservative pressure, President Clinton promised to "end welfare as we know it" (Congressional Research Service, 2001) and transformed AFDC into the Temporary Assistance for Needy Families (TANF) program which imposed five-year lifetime limits and strict work requirements. The goals of the Personal Responsibility and Work Opportunity Reconciliation Act of 1996, which authorized TANF, were explicit:

(1) provide assistance to needy families so that children may be cared for in their own homes or in the homes of relatives;
(2) end the dependence of needy parents on government benefits by promoting job preparation, work, and marriage;
(3) prevent and reduce the incidence of out-of-wedlock pregnancies and establish annual numerical goals for preventing and reducing the incidence of these pregnancies; and
(4) encourage the formation and maintenance of two-parent families (Personal Responsibility and Work Opportunity Reconciliation Act, 1996).

One might notice that the policy does not include the goals of eradicating poverty or improving outcomes for children, except in that it seeks to reduce costly out-of-home placements. The result of this new focus has been dramatic. While 80.5% of children in poverty received AFDC in 1973 (Piven & Cloward, 1993), only 16% of poor children received TANF in 2016 (Child Trends, 2018). Meanwhile, the Food Stamps program (now called the Supplemental Nutrition Assistance Program or SNAP) has grown considerably, arguably as a way to give the government greater control over how aid is spent.

Where We Stand Today

The compounding effects of declining wages in America and the dismantling of the welfare state have had a devastating impact on low-income American families. In 2017, 12.3% of all Americans or 39.7 million people lived below the US Census Bureau's official poverty measure (US Census Bureau, 2018b). These numbers likely do not paint the full picture, however. The US Department of Agriculture developed the official measure in the 1960s, when the average American household spent roughly a third of its budget on food. To this day, poverty is measured by taking the cost of a minimally nutritious food budget and tripling it. But this is not how family budgets work today. Rising housing costs, especially in major cities, have far outpaced the cost of food. The Supplemental Poverty Measure of 2010 better reflects modern budgets and geographic differences in cost of living but has yet to replace the official poverty threshold. By this measure, 14% of the population lived in poverty in 2016, a difference of roughly 5.5 million people (US Census Bureau, 2018a). Further, the rise of "deep poverty" or those earning less than 50% of the official poverty threshold is troubling. The number of children living in households with less than $2 per person, per day—the World Bank's official definition of extreme global poverty—tripled between 1995 and 2012 (Shaefer & Edin, 2018).

We also know that the gap between the rich and the poor has grown significantly in recent decades. In 2015, households in the top 1% earned 26.3 times the average household in the bottom 99% (Sommeiller & Price, 2018). This extreme level of inequality has not always been the case. The Economy Policy Institute reports an interesting trend in wages among the 1% and the 99% between 1945 and 2007.

> The average inflation-adjusted income of the bottom 99 percent of families grew by 100.1 percent between 1945 and 1973. Over the same period, the average income of the top 1 percent of families grew by 34.3 percent. Faster income growth for the bottom 99 percent of families meant that the top 1 percent captured just 4.9 percent of all income growth over the period… The pattern in the distribution of income growth reversed itself from 1973 to 2007 as the income of the bottom 99 percent of families grew much more slowly (by just 15.4 percent) compared with the top 1 percent, whose average income grew by 216.4 percent. As a result, over half (58.7 percent) of all income growth in this period landed in the hands of the top 1 percent of families. (Sommeiller & Price, 2018)

By 2007, it took the average worker in the bottom 90% one year to earn what the richest 0.1% earn in a day and a half (Stiglitz, 2012). In case the growth of children living in America on less than $2 per day does not cause sufficient alarm, this should: income inequality is bad for the entire economy. The Organization for Economic Cooperation and Development (OECD) estimates that income inequality between the 1980s and the Great Recession cost the United States 6–9% in GDP growth (Cingano, 2014). This loss can largely be explained by the laws of supply and demand. High and low earners tend to respond differently to an increase in income (either through increased wages, tax cuts, government transfers, or investment dividends): people who don't need the extra money tend to save it and people who do need the money tend to spend it (Stiglitz, 2012). When low-income families spend money, it creates a demand for more goods, which then creates more economic growth and jobs.

Many factors drive American inequality: declining investment in education, falling median income, globalization, and the growth of technology. In the 1960s, for example, a family of three could be lifted above the poverty line with one member working full-time at the minimum wage (Piven & Cloward, 1993). But the OECD and progressive economists like Joseph Stiglitz argue that "Cash transfers and increasing access to public services, such as high-quality education, training and healthcare, are an essential social investment to create greater equality of opportunities in the long run…provided these policies are well designed, targeted and implemented" (Organization for Economic Cooperation and Development, 2014). The focus of this book is whether our current social safety net is actually "well designed."

Even though 17% of the average American's income now comes from government programs such as TANF, SNAP, and Social Security, surveys have found that the perception of welfare as something that facilitates idleness has only grown in recent decades (Badger, 2018). The word "welfare" itself has pejorative connotations for many. At their most generous, Americans like to think of the welfare system as a temporary leg up to those experiencing a financial setback. But as we have discussed, this has never been the case. Social welfare has always been intended to subdue discontent without harming the labor supply and was never designed to foster financial mobility. Therefore, American skepticism in social welfare programs may not be entirely off base. This book will explore a growing body of research which suggests that eligibility rules in our current poverty programs exacerbate inequality and contribute to economic stagnation.

In the following chapters, I will discuss outcome data for our current poverty alleviation programs alongside a Universal Basic Income (UBI), which has recently gained renewed interest in policy circles. For several reasons, UBI is seen by advocates as an idea whose time has finally come. Firstly, the Great Recession of 2008 awakened many Americans, for the first time in nearly a century, to the unreliable nature of capitalist markets. Pendulum swings in the global market bring both unprecedented wealth in times of growth and devastation to millions when economies decline. In the richest country on Earth, we have the resources to ensure that citizens have their most basic needs met regardless of the ebb and flow of our economic system.

Further, technological advancements, especially Artificial Intelligence (AI), threaten to replace many low wage workers. Unlike the relentless demand for labor created by agriculture and manufacturing in America's early years, AI has the potential to replace large sectors of modern workers from fast food service to manufacturing and trucking. Depending on the study you cite, it will replace anywhere from 9% to 50% of the US labor force (Arntz, Gregory, & Zierahn, 2016; Frey & Osborne, 2017). Even if AI does not replace all low wage jobs, it will increase competition for the jobs that remain, further suppressing wages. Finally, the rise of the "gig economy," in which workers provide piecemeal contract labor, has increased convenience for all of us (via apps like Uber and TaskRabbit) but means that many workers lack benefits and steady incomes.

The resurgence of interest in UBI has inspired the implementation of multiple pilot demonstrations around the world, a handful of which are taking place in North America. The Silicon Valley investment group, Y Combinator, is in the planning stages of a pilot which will provide $1000 per month to 3000 recipients for three to five years (Y Combinator, 2017). The City of Stockton, California, launched a randomized control trial in early 2019 with 100 residents in low-income neighborhoods receiving $500 per month for 18 months (Martin-West, Baker, Balakrishnan, Rao, & You, 2018). The Magnolia Mother's Trust provided 16 low-income black mothers in Jackson, Mississippi with $1000 per month for 12 months, with no conditions (Coehlo, 2018).

As in the 1970s, one of the largest basic income pilots occurred in Canada. More than 4000 Ontario residents began receiving approximately $1415 CA monthly for individuals and $2002 CA for couples (recipients with disabilities receive an additional $500 per month) in early 2017 (Ontario Ministry of Children, Community and Social Services, 2017). A control group of 2000 was also recruited, lending important credibility. However, in Fall 2018, a new conservative government was elected in Ontario who quickly announced the early closure of the pilot. It is still unclear whether and how data will be collected. The Ontario Basic Income Network gathered surveys with a sub-sample of 424 participants to ensure that at least some amount of data could be preserved (Basic Income Canada Network, 2019). Further, I completed in-depth interviews with several Ontario basic income recipients, all of whom had previously received some form of traditional welfare.

Despite this book's title, our current social safety net does "work" by some calculations. The Food Stamp program alone lifts 8.4 million people above the poverty line every year and reduces the childhood poverty rate by 28% (Wheaton & Tran, n.d.). While these families may be raised just above the poverty threshold, I will argue that counterproductive modern welfare rules do little to create true economic mobility and may even exacerbate it. While 90% of children born in 1940 out earned their parents, only 50% born in the 1980s will do so (Chetty et al., 2017). Today, the strongest predictor of an American child's future economic success is that of his parents. Even if low-income children outperform rich kids in school, they are still less likely to be financially successful (Stiglitz, 2012). Further, welfare programs reach only a fraction of families in need; less than a quarter of low-income families received TANF assistance in 2017 (Floyd, Pavetti, & Schott, 2015).

American capitalism has made us the most prosperous nation in the world, and this book is in no way a proposal to dismantle that. It does not seek to cap CEO wages—even though they are currently 271 times the average worker's salary—or make a turn toward socialism (Mishel & Schieder, 2017). Proposals that American capitalists simply seek lower profits may be naive. It is in the best interest of anyone with a stock-based retirement portfolio to ensure that publicly traded companies produce healthy returns. Capitalism is quickly collapsing from within, however, if there are not enough people to buy the goods we produce, if children are raised in deprivation and are then unable to meaningfully contribute to the workforce as adults, and if the social safety net is actually a trap. In this book, I will explore basic income as a way to shore up rather than replace capitalism.

On the other hand, this book is in no way meant to provide support for libertarian proposals to replace "Social Security, Medicare, Medicaid, food stamps, Supplemental Security Income, housing subsidies, welfare for single women and every other kind of welfare and social-services program, as well as agricultural subsidies and corporate welfare" (Murray, 2016) with one basic income payment. Health care costs alone would swallow the $13,000 per year that he proposes and leave low-income families much worse off. Further, geographic differences in housing costs would make the full removal of subsidies like Section 8 disastrous. If we want people to drive buses and serve food in major cities, we need to make sure they can afford to live there. For vastly different reasons, I may agree with Mr. Murray, however, on the replacement of some cash assistance programs. Too many low-income families describe the experience of "hustling backward" in which any attempt to improve their lives, such as accepting small raises or extra hours, only worsens the situation when punitive and restrictive welfare rules leave them worse off financially. As one basic income recipient in Ontario told me, "You survive social assistance, [but] I became a human again under basic income."

References

Abramovitz, M. (1996). *Regulating the Lives of Women: Social Welfare Policy from Colonial Times to the Present.* Boston: South End Press.

Arntz, M., Gregory, T., & Zierahn, U. (2016). *The Risk of Automation for Jobs in OECD Countries.* https://doi.org/10.1787/5jlz9h56dvq7-en.

Badger, E. (2018, August 7). The Outsize Hold of the Word 'Welfare' on the Public Imagination. *The New York Times.* Retrieved from https://www.nytimes.com/2018/08/06/upshot/welfare-and-the-public-imagination.html

Basic Income Canada Network. (2019). *Signposts to Success: Report of a BICN Survey of Ontario Basic Income Recipients.* Retrieved from Basic Income Canada Network Website: https://www.basicincomecanada.org/time_for_national_action_new_report_shows_ontario_basic_income_pilot_was_on_track_to_success?fbclid=IwAR1BcwCr6pQ-kLHv_YRXddbK48jv2OLH9pGX-X1rU_946RB-Kvro2wvVrCg

Basic Income Earth Network. (2018). *History of Basic Income.* Retrieved October 27, 2018, from BIEN Website: http://basicincome.org/basic-income/history/

Bell, W., & Bushe, D. M. (1975). The Economic Efficiency of AFDC. *Social Service Review, 49*(2), 175–190.

Chetty, R., Grusky, D., Hell, M., Hendren, N., Manduca, R., & Narang, J. (2017). The Fading American Dream: Trends in Absolute Income Mobility Since 1940. *Science, 356*(6336), 398–406. https://doi.org/10.1126/science.aal4617.

Child Trends. (2018). *Child Recipients of Welfare (AFDC/TANF).* Retrieved from Child Trends Website: https://www.childtrends.org/indicators/child-recipients-of-welfareafdctanf

Cingano, F. (2014). *Trends in Income Inequality and Its Impact on Economic Growth.* Retrieved from Organisation for Economic Cooperation and Development Website: https://www.oecd-ilibrary.org/social-issues-migration-health/trends-in-income-inequality-and-its-impact-on-economic-growth_5jxrjncwxv6j-en

Coehlo, A. (2018, November 11). *United States: The Magnolia Mother's Trust Innovates and Starts a Basic Income-Like Experiment with African American Women.* Retrieved January 7, 2019, from Basic Income News Website: http://basicincome.org/news/2018/11/united-states-the-magnolia-mothers-trust-innovates-and-starts-a-basic-income-like-experiment-with-african-american-women/

Congressional Research Service. (2001). *Short History of the 1996 Welfare Reform Law* (No. RS20807; p. 7). Retrieved from https://www.everycrsreport.com/files/20010207_RS20807_c9b18070b6269eac37d3074ab721fa53dcdeb4cc.pdf

Floyd, I., Pavetti, L., & Schott, L. (2015). *TANF Reaching Few Poor Families.* Retrieved from Center for Budget Policies and Priorities Website: https://www.cbpp.org/research/family-income-support/tanf-reaching-few-poor-families

Frey, C. B., & Osborne, M. A. (2017). The Future of Employment: How Susceptible Are Jobs to Computerisation? *Technological Forecasting and Social Change, 114,* 254–280. https://doi.org/10.1016/j.techfore.2016.08.019.

Friedman, M. (2009). *Capitalism and Freedom: Fortieth Anniversary Edition.* Chicago: University of Chicago Press.

Gooden, S., & Douglas, N. (2006). Ever Present, Sometimes Acknowledged, But Never Addressed: Racial Disparities in U.S. Welfare Policy. In K. Kilty & E. Segal (Eds.), *The Promise of Welfare Reform: Political Rhetoric and Reality of Poverty in the Twenty-First Century* (pp. 207–222). New York: Hawthorne.

Green, C. M. (2015). *Secret City: A History of Race Relations in the Nation's Capital.* Princeton, NJ: Princeton University Press.

Hahn, H., Aron, L. Y., Lou, C., Pratt, E., & Okoli, A. (2017). *Why Does Cash Welfare Depend on Where You Live?* Retrieved from Urban Institute Website: https://www.urban.org/research/publication/why-does-cash-welfare-depend-where-you-live

Isenberg, N. (2017). *White Trash: The 400-Year Untold History of Class in America* (Reprint ed.). New York: Penguin Books.

Jansson, B. S. (2014). *The Reluctant Welfare State: Engaging History to Advance Social Work Practice in Contemporary Society* (8th ed.). Belmont, CA: Cengage Learning.

Joseph, A. (2006). Welfare Reform: Forward to the Past. In K. Kilty & E. Segal (Eds.), *The Promise of Welfare Reform: Political Rhetoric and Reality of Poverty in the Twenty-First Century* (pp. 39–47). New York: Hawthorne.

Katz, A. J. (1973). Four Income Maintenance Experiments. *Social Work, 18*(2), 4–113. Retrieved from JSTOR.

King, M. L., Jr. (2010). *Where Do We Go from Here: Chaos or Community?* Boston: Beacon Press.

Levin, J. (2013, December 19). *The Real Story of Linda Taylor, America's Original Welfare Queen*. Retrieved January 1, 2019, from Slate Magazine Website: http://www.slate.com/articles/news_and_politics/history/2013/12/linda_taylor_welfare_queen_ronald_reagan_made_her_a_notorious_american_villain.html

Levin, J. (2019). *The Queen: The Forgotten Life Behind an American Myth*. New York: Little, Brown and Company.

Marinescu, I. (2017). *No Strings Attached: The Behavioral Effects of U.S. Unconditional Cash Transfer Programs*. Retrieved from Roosevelt Institute Website: http://rooseveltinstitute.org/wp-content/uploads/2017/05/No-Strings-Attached-050417-1.pdf

Martin-West, S., Baker, A. C., Balakrishnan, S., Rao, K., & You, G. (2018). *Pre-Analysis Plan: Stockton Economic Empowerment Demonstration* (p. 11). Retrieved from https://static1.squarespace.com/static/59d55793268b96ccff4ff70e/t/5c0eb980575d1fbc6d9996ed/1544468865166/SEED_PaP_V2+%281%29.pdf

Mishel, L., & Schieder, J. (2017). *CEO Pay Remains High Relative to the Pay of Typical Workers and High-Wage Earners* (p. 25). Retrieved from Economic Policy Institute Website: https://www.epi.org/files/pdf/130354.pdf

More, T. (2003). *Utopia* (Reissue ed.; P. Turner, Ed.). London/New York: Penguin Classics.

Murray, C. (2016, June 3). *Universal Income: A Guaranteed Income for Every American*. Retrieved January 28, 2019, from American Enterprise Institute Website: http://www.aei.org/publication/a-guaranteed-income-for-every-american/

Ontario Ministry of Children, Community and Social Services. (2017, April 24). *Ontario Basic Income Pilot | Ontario.ca*. Retrieved April 11, 2019, from https://www.ontario.ca/page/ontario-basic-income-pilot

Organization for Economic Cooperation and Development. (2014, September 12). *Inequality Hurts Economic Growth, Finds OECD Research—OECD*. Retrieved January 4, 2019, from http://www.oecd.org/newsroom/inequality-hurts-economic-growth.htm

Personal Responsibility and Work Opportunity Reconciliation Act of 1996. Pub. L. No. 104–193, 42 601 42 USC 601 (1996).

Piven, F. F., & Cloward, R. (1993). *Regulating the Poor: The Functions of Public Welfare* (Updated, Subsequent ed.). New York: Vintage.

Roosevelt, F. (1935). *Annual Message to Congress*. Retrieved December 18, 2018, from The American Presidency Project Website: https://www.presidency.ucsb.edu/documents/annual-message-congress-3

Russell, B. (2013). *Proposed Roads to Freedom: Socialism, Anarchism, and Syndicalism*. Los Angeles, CA: HardPress Publishing.

Shaefer, H. L., & Edin, K. (2018). *Welfare Reform and the Families It Left Behind* (pp. 22–27). Retrieved from Stanford Center on Poverty & Inequality Website: https://inequality.stanford.edu/sites/default/files/Pathways_Winter2018_Families-Left-Behind.pdf

Social Security Administration. (2018). *Legislative History of the Social Security Disability Program*. Retrieved from https://www.ssa.gov/legislation/DI%20legislative%20history.pdf

Sommeiller, E., & Price, M. (2018). *The New Gilded Age: Income Inequality in the U.S. By State, Metropolitan Area, and County*. Retrieved from Economic Policy Institute Website: https://www.epi.org/publication/the-new-gilded-age-income-inequality-in-the-u-s-by-state-metropolitan-area-and-county/

Soss, J., Fording, R. C., & Schram, S. F. (2008). The Color of Devolution: Race, Federalism, and the Politics of Social Control. *American Journal of Political Science, 52*(3), 536–553. https://doi.org/10.1111/j.1540-5907.2008.00328.x.

Standing, G. (2017). *Basic Income: A Guide for the Open-Minded*. New Haven, CT/London: Yale University Press.

Stiglitz, J. E. (2012). *The Price of Inequality: How Today's Divided Society Endangers Our Future* (1st ed.). New York: W. W. Norton & Company.

US Census Bureau. (2018a). *How the U.S. Census Bureau Measures Poverty*. Retrieved January 1, 2019, from https://www.census.gov/library/visualizations/2017/demo/poverty_measure-how.html

US Census Bureau. (2018b). *Income and Poverty in the United States: 2017*. Retrieved January 1, 2019, from https://www.census.gov/library/publications/2018/demo/p60-263.html

Vives, J. L. (2002). *De Subventione Pauperum Sive de Humanis Necessitatibus*. Leiden, Netherlands: Brill.

Wheaton, L., & Tran, V. (n.d.). *The Antipoverty Effects of the Supplemental Nutrition Assistance Program* (p. 52). Retrieved from Urban Institute Website: https://www.urban.org/sites/default/files/publication/96521/the_antipoverty_effects_of_the_supplemental_nutrition_assistance_program_3.pdf

Withorn, A. (2006). Looking Up the Slippery Slope: Lessons from a Lifetime of Trying to Figure Out and Fight Poverty. In K. Kilty & E. Segal (Eds.), *The Promise of Welfare Reform: Political Rhetoric and the Reality of Poverty in the Twenty-First Century* (pp. 7–21). New York: The Hawthorne Press.

Y Combinator. (2017). *Basic Income Project Proposal: Overview for Comments and Feedback*. Retrieved from https://static1.squarespace.com/static/599c23b2e6f2e1aeb8d35ec6/t/59c3188c4c326da3497c355f/1505958039366/YCR-Basic-Income-Proposal.pdf

CHAPTER 2

From Welfare to Work (In Theory)

Abstract The primary goal of the modern American welfare state is to move recipients to employment and independence as quickly as possible. Fears of generational welfare dependency motivated the implementation of Welfare Reform in 1996. The evidence is overwhelming, however, that this approach has only exacerbated poverty and its societal consequences. Trusting all people, including those with low-incomes, to make their own work, family, and financial decisions has a transformative effect on recipients and the communities around them. Universal basic income pilots have discovered little, if any, changes to employment among recipients, improved physical and mental health, better employment prospects, and increased community economic productivity.

Keywords Employment • TANF work requirements • TANF sanctions

To fully understand the logic of the American welfare system, it helps to consider the significant influence of capitalism and the high cultural value we place on it. The delicate dance between welfare and the labor market is reinforced in multiple ways. Firstly, since the market-based economy's early European roots, it has been in the best interests of businesses to ensure that welfare is never more attractive than low-wage work (Abramovitz, 2006). This concept of "less eligibility" was first made explicit in the British Poor Reform Act of 1834, stating that the conditions

L. Hamilton, *Welfare Doesn't Work*, Exploring the Basic Income Guarantee, https://doi.org/10.1007/978-3-030-37121-0_2

of public assistance must always be worse than the lowest paid job (Blau, 2006). Interestingly, this concept has also been applied to prison design for hundreds of years to ensure that the conditions of imprisonment are worse than that afforded to the poorest free citizen (Sieh, 1989).

It is also critical to the stability of capitalism that citizens genuinely believe in the inherent value of work, both morally and practically. People must believe that the capitalist system will reward their hard work and that those unwilling to work are immoral. To reinforce that one must prove themselves "deserving" of aid through hard work, early relief workhouses, established in England in 1723, required the poor to provide labor in return for assistance (Piven & Cloward, 1993). Some early American charities, such as the Charity Organization Societies, likewise required labor in return for a place to sleep and a meal (Blau, 2006).

Western social policy has also traditionally been designed to ensure that there is always a greater supply of low-skilled workers than low-skill jobs. The laws of supply and demand state that when there is a larger supply of workers than jobs (demand), employers can offer lower wages. Economists refer to this rule as the Phillips Curve. When there are more low-skill workers than low-skill jobs, wages can be kept low and profits high. As an early example, during the Black Plague of Europe, a worker shortage put leverage in the hands of peasants that had scarcely existed before. To regain control and ensure that workers would continue to work for low wages, laws were passed in the mid-1300s in England that created punishment for almsgiving (giving money to beggars), instituted *maximum* wages, and made it illegal for peasants to move in search of higher wages (Piven & Cloward, 1993).

The modern American government has made arguably similar efforts to ensure a steady stream of workers. As the growth of American industry demanded greater numbers of cheap laborers, willing to work in hazardous conditions, in 1824, the state of New York barred working-age males from receiving public assistance (Blau, 2006). Then, in 1873, the New York State Pauper Act expanded aid to the disabled but reiterated again that able-bodied males were excluded.

During the Great Depression, many American business owners were unhappy with FDR's federal work relief plans such as the Works Progress Administration and the Civilian Conservation Corps as it made workers less desperate and therefore less willing to accept any wage offered. They exerted pressure on the federal government to close these programs as the economy slowly recovered (Piven & Cloward, 1993). In a compromise with industry, federal relief programs intentionally offered a lower wage than the private sector to ensure that private employment was always more attractive.

The Role of Minority Labor

Here again, we cannot discuss the relationship between labor and welfare without understanding the significant influence of America's institutionalized racism. For example, when Social Security was first established in 1935, it specifically excluded agricultural and domestic workers, two fields dominated by black and Latino Americans. The American economy, especially in the South, relied heavily on the exploitation of minority labor and significant efforts were made to ensure that black and Latino workers had few alternatives.

In the heavily racialized tenant farming economy of the South, black workers lived in shacks on the plantation and were charged high rents against their meager wages. As a result, tenant farmers were often in debt to their employers and trapped indefinitely, resulting in an exploitative labor relationship not entirely unlike slavery (Piven & Cloward, 1993). Southern Congressman advocated for local administration of New Deal relief programs, which Piven and Cloward (1993, p. 115) argue allowed for the continuance of "the caste economy of the South." As a result, in the 1940s and '50s, southern welfare offices offered much lower monthly grants than northern states (averaging $8.10 per month in Arkansas and $61.07 in Massachusetts in 1939) (Piven & Cloward, 1993) and simply closed during cotton and tobacco harvests to ensure that black workers had little choice but to accept any wages offered (Abramovitz, 2006). One Southern welfare manager in the 1930s was explicit about the rationale for this approach (Larbee, 1939, p. 454).

> The number of Negro cases is few due to the unanimous feeling on the part of the staff and board that there are more work opportunities for Negro women and to their intense desire not to interfere with local labor conditions. The attitude that they have always gotten along, and that "all they'll do is have more children" [if given welfare] is definite...There is hesitancy on the part of lay boards to advance too rapidly over the thinking of their own communities, which see no reason why the employable Negro mother should not continue her usually sketchy seasonal labor or indefinite domestic service rather than receive a public assistance grant.

This disparity continued for decades. In 1961, in rural areas, the average AFDC grant to white families was $21.90 and $11.70 to black families. As late as the 1960s, AFDC was cut off during harvest season, with the assumption that recipients could find work in the fields. These policies achieved their intended effect: nearly twice as many black mothers continued to work while receiving aid than white mothers (Piven & Cloward, 1993).

Mechanization and Globalization

Several developments in the 1950s and '60s moved American businesses away from its former dependence upon human labor. First, as farm technology rapidly expanded, the demand for agricultural labor declined. While mechanization increased farm productivity by 45% between 1950 and 1965, it decreased agricultural employment by the same proportion. Then, the first federal minimum wage was set at $1.00 per hour in 1966, creating even greater pressure on employers to mechanize (Piven & Cloward, 1993). Finally, in the 1970s, Germany and Japan began to threaten America's place as a leader in manufacturing, further incentivizing American businesses to decrease labor costs (Blau, 2006).

Interestingly, the social safety net can also influence the previously discussed Phillips Curve. In the 1960s and '70s unemployment increased, but wages did not decline as predicted. Analysts believed that the expansion of welfare benefits during this time gave workers greater bargaining power (Piven & Cloward, 1993). In response, corporate America began pushing a narrative of smaller government, which included removing regulations put in place after the Depression, less powerful unions, lower taxes, and fewer public programs. Their efforts were incredibly successful. In 1970, 29.1% of American workers belonged to a union. By 1990, this number had fallen to 12% (Piven & Cloward, 1993). Unions, public programs, and government regulations had ensured that, between 1949 and 1980, as America's economy grew, workers benefited. Wages and national productivity increased at generally the same rate (Stiglitz, 2012). But deregulation in the 1970s and '80s quickly began to decouple economic productivity and worker welfare.

In the 1990s, amid globalization and outsourcing of labor, corporate America suddenly had many more cards in their hands. American workers were no longer in competition with each other, but with the entire world. Even while the American economy expanded, "a heightened sense of job insecurity" among workers was sufficient to keep wages low according to Federal Reserve Chairman Alan Greenspan (Federal Reserve Board, 1997). As the real value of the minimum wage and median wage declined, welfare had to become even less attractive. In order to accomplish this, Piven and Cloward (1993, p. 148) argue that politicians created a successful distraction from growing inequality by pointing at "welfare queens" as the real problem with America. Two age-old and mutually reinforcing narratives proved useful to these ends: that "economic success is a matter of individual merit" and "those who fail—the very poor—are therefore morally or personally defective."

Welfare "Reform": Work Requirements, Sanctions, and Other Bad Ideas

The solution to growing fears of generational welfare dependency and workforce separation was to "end welfare as we know it" and transform the Aid to Families with Dependent Children program into Temporary Assistance to Needy Families (TANF) via the Personal Responsibility and Work Opportunity Reconciliation Act of 1996. As a compromise between President Clinton and increasing conservatism in Congress, "Welfare Reform" implemented five-year lifetime limits and 24 months in any one stint. States are free to set lower limits (the lowest being 12 months in Arizona). States can also create work requirements and sanctions for TANF recipients, a policy which has been proposed for replication in the SNAP and Medicaid programs (Booker, 2018).

With the establishment of TANF, the expectation that recipients move into employment as quickly as possible became explicit, even though the Economic Policy Institute predicted that pushing TANF recipients into the workforce would depress wages for all low-income workers (via increased competition) by an average of 10% (Abramovitz, 1996). States are required to meet work participation rates, meaning that a certain percentage of the TANF caseload must work, volunteer, or participate in training programs. In most cases, the target rate is 50% (Lower-Basch, 2018). To meet this requirement, many states implemented "welfare to work" programs that seek to transition welfare recipients to employment.

These efforts were nothing new, however. As early as the 1960s, work incentive programs were introduced under AFDC. The Work Incentive Now program of 1967 removed the dollar for dollar deduction of welfare benefits (in other words, benefits decreasing by a dollar for every dollar earned through employment) and replaced it with a more gradual decrease. The program also offered employment support services such as job training, child care, and transportation assistance. These programs failed because most welfare recipients had significant personal barriers to gainful employment, and those that did find work rarely made more than welfare payments (Gold, 1971). Further, work programs reduced the number of job openings for other workers. Ultimately, the programs closed as they were found to be more expensive than simply providing cash assistance (Piven & Cloward, 1993).

Nonetheless, the failure of previous welfare to work programs did little to dissuade the architects of TANF from another attempt. The primary difference is that, unlike AFDC, TANF is not an entitlement program, meaning that even if families are legitimately unable to find work and meet the eligibility criteria for assistance, they have no statutory right to it. This loophole has allowed the program to push otherwise eligible families off the welfare rolls when they reach the time limit or through "sanctions" for non-compliance, which are often minor offenses such as not completing a form correctly or being unable to jump through the administrative hoops set before applicants. Seefeldt (2017, p. 13) describes the case of "Ginger," a woman with a disability facing these types of hurdles in her state's job training program, "Work First."

> She had applied for disability benefits through the federal Supplemental Security Income (SSI) program, and had been denied, but was appealing the decision. While she was waiting for her case to work its way through the appeal process, she was receiving TANF. At first, her pending disability application exempted her from attending Work First. Then the state changed its policy with respect to SSI applicants, and Ginger was told she needed to start going. Carless, Ginger would have needed to walk to a bus stop in order to get to the program site. Her physical limitations left her unable to do that. Rather than assist with transportation, the welfare office stopped Ginger's TANF benefits.

Ginger was left to survive on housing assistance and Food Stamps until her disability benefits were approved and traded sexual favors in return for items that Food Stamps didn't cover, such as toilet paper. The ultimate and arguably intentional result of work requirements, sanctions, and time limits is that assistance budgets can remain low, with no accountability for whether families actually attain economic independence when they leave the program. Low budgets are good news for federal and state governments, as TANF provides funds via block grants to states, which means that each state gets a set amount of money annually, regardless of fluctuations in their caseloads, national economic conditions (such as a recession), or inflation. States were also given the freedom to use the TANF block grant on a wide range of services, including transportation, child care, and work preparation. In practice, many states have shifted these block grant funds into other struggling programs such as child welfare services, Head Start, and low-income tax credits. Today, only about half of TANF block grants actually go to TANF services, and less than a quarter is spent on direct cash assistance to families (Center on Budget and Policy Priorities, 2019).

Seefeldt (2017) argues that in an era of diminishing revenues, a stagnant TANF block grant ($16.5 billion for every year since 1996) (Center on Budget and Policy Priorities, 2015), and required work participation rates, states are incentivized to focus their efforts on clients who are more easily moved to employment and quietly push clients with more complex needs (low levels of education, disabilities, and health complications) off the program. A TANF program manager in another study echoed the concern that counties are incentivized to prioritize moving clients off of the program as quickly as possible—rather than providing the best possible services to the client—because counties face their own financial sanctions for not meeting required work participation rates (Gross, Church, Taylor, & Towne-Roese, 2018).

Ultimately, the strongest predictor of a TANF recipient's long-term success is their previous education and work experience rather than any intervention services they might receive while on the program (Ybarra & Noyes, 2019). A study of 60 welfare "leavers" in Georgia found that less than 20% were actually economically self-sufficient (Brooks, Mack, Chaney, Gibson, & Caplan, 2018). A handful of states, such as Massachusetts and California, have opted to loosen their work requirements and allow recipients to keep more of their wages before losing benefits, with incredible results. In these states, TANF recipients move to higher wage, higher benefit work when they leave the program, even if it takes them a little longer to become self-sufficient (Lim, Coulton, & Lalich, 2009). In other words, when recipients are given the breathing room to search for a good job, rather than pressured to take the first one that comes along, they are more likely to become financially independent in the long run. Unfortunately, these states are not the norm. Nationwide,

TANF program data reveal that far more families leave the program due to reaching time limits than obtaining gainful employment (Zedlewski, 2016).

Work requirements do, however, effectively leave workers vulnerable to exploitation because participants know that benefits can terminate if they refuse a job offer, are fired, or quit. One recipient in a job placement program told researchers that she was let go and then lost both TANF and SNAP after refusing to complete extra work after her shift had ended (Black & Sprague, 2017).

> In one [job] placement as a teacher's assistant at a private school, "Carla" was fired after declining when she was asked at the end of her shift if she "felt like cleaning the bathroom"—a duty that was not included in the job description. "I really think it was just to see how far she could push me, just how much you could take from me to degrade me. You know what I'm saying? Just, 'How much will she take before she act like how I think she should act?'"

The macroeconomic context for TANF work requirements includes declining well-paid, medium-skilled jobs and increasing poverty wage, service sector employment (Shapiro, 2017). A social services manager in Ohio told researchers that their department struggled to move TANF recipients to employment because there were simply not enough jobs and that clients often faced significant personal barriers which made it difficult to be competitive for the jobs that existed (Taylor, Gross, & Towne-Roese, 2016). In qualitative interviews with former TANF recipients in Michigan, Seefeldt (2017, pp. 11–12) found that most respondents described job training programs as a "waste of time," and the real problem was a lack of available jobs. One respondent stated that "sometimes the [work preparation] instructors would just not do anything. I mean, we were just sitting there, just having our own conversations. That would be for a week's time." Still, this program allows the state to meet its "work participation rate" because these recipients were receiving work preparation "training." There are currently no mechanisms for ensuring that these programs are either effective or efficient. Work requirements are especially harmful to African American families who are statistically more likely to lack a high school education and still face significant discrimination in the workplace. As a result, minority recipients are less likely to find a job before reaching the time limit, less likely to stay off welfare permanently, and less likely to escape poverty (Schram, 2006).

In addition to discrimination, declining job availability, and personal challenges like low education, TANF families face the competing demands of parenthood and work experienced by all working parents. TANF work requirements can tip the scales of this balance from difficult to impossible. For example, some states require TANF mothers who give birth to return to work more quickly than others. Mothers remain dependent on welfare longer when they are mandated to go back to work shortly after giving birth. Researchers hypothesized that pushing women to employment so quickly makes it more difficult for mothers to find well-paid work that can sustain their family in the long term. Instead, they are more likely to take low paying, unreliable jobs to meet work requirements (Kim, 2018).

Sometimes women are unable to take jobs simply because they cannot afford or find quality child care (Blau, 2006). Child care subsidies, which are associated with better educational outcomes for children (Marshall, Robeson, Tracy, Frye, & Roberts, 2013) and higher employment rates for low-income women (Ahn, 2012), are in decline (Pew Charitable Trusts, 2016). Only about one in ten eligible children currently receive subsidized child care (Madill, 2017). Further, long subsidy waitlists often mean that families are left to pay out of pocket for childcare if they are to remain compliant with TANF work requirements (Marshall et al., 2013).

Not surprisingly, work requirements and other bureaucratic hurdles create a great deal of stress for TANF families. Unemployed TANF recipients report worse mental health outcomes than even similarly poor, unemployed people who do not receive TANF (Cheng, 2007). This stress and financial precarity also has significant repercussions for the physical health of recipients. Post 1996 "Welfare Reform" is associated with decreased healthcare utilization and an increased likelihood of being unable to afford needed care among the poor (Bitler, Gelbach, & Hoynes, 2005). When people are ill, unable to access treatment, and therefore unable to work, the entire economy is affected (World Health Organization, 2009). According to the Centers for Disease Control (2019), chronic and untreated diseases cost the economy hundreds of billions per year in lost wages and economic productivity.

Welfare sanctions (reductions in TANF payments for a range of non-compliant behavior) are also associated with significant negative outcomes for participants. Sanctions depress the wage growth of TANF recipients, presumably because even a small financial setback can have disastrous effects for a family already experiencing economic precarity. For example, a modest reduction in payments might make the difference in the ability to afford reliable transportation to work or childcare, further harming the family's ability to become self-sufficient (Fording, Schram, & Soss, 2013). One TANF recipient told researchers that sanctions for not being able to meet TANF requirements during her children's hospital stays for asthma attacks caused her to miss rent payments and led to eviction twice (Hildebrandt, 2016). Rather than motivating a recipient to remain compliant with TANF rules, sanctions push recipients off of TANF more quickly, even if the family has no job or a job that pays less than welfare benefits (Wu, Cancian, & Wallace, 2014). And again, there appears to be a racist component at play. Black and Latina women are more likely to receive TANF work-related sanctions than white women (Monnat, 2010).

Finally, low-income limits for TANF eligibility, while intended to ensure assistance only for the very needy, are found to create negative incentives for recipients. The welfare "Cliff Effect" occurs when a family suddenly loses all benefits when receiving even a small increase in income. Unlike the 1960s, a gradual "stepping down" of benefits to encourage employment is now relatively unusual. Families are often left in a worse financial condition when accepting a small raise or promotion as they may lose TANF, SNAP, housing assistance, and child care assistance all at once (Minton & Durham, 2013; Roll & East, 2014). Many families simply turn down promotional opportunities or extra hours at work if it means they would be unable to feed their children or afford quality child care. One TANF recipient, "Doreen," exemplifies this trap (Seccombe, Walters, & James, 1999, p. 201).

> Doreen, a 31-year-old African American woman, who receives welfare for herself, and her pregnant 15-year-old daughter, said that she would like to get a job, and has earnestly looked for work in the past, but usually can only find part-time pay in the fast food industry. Accepting this type of employment causes her to lose her medical insurance, and most of her welfare assistance. So, instead, she baby-sits occasionally for extra money, and does not report this pay to her caseworker.

These disincentives are not unique to TANF. One MTurker who previously received SNAP told me that "the requirements were preposterous and it made it so getting a low wage job was detrimental." Another explained that "I would have been kicked off immediate *[sic]* if I went back to school. I would have been kicked off if I accepted anything more than a minimum wage job. It was frustrating."

Conservative politicians are well aware of the so-called "welfare trap." They often cite stories like Doreen's to illustrate why, in their belief, welfare should be made more challenging to receive and provide fewer benefits. Such stories often stoke support for legislative attempts to "crack down" on welfare dependence. But as the data illustrates, again and again, these efforts make it even more difficult for low-income families to get ahead. When we relax welfare rules and give families space to get on their feet, actual progress can occur. What if this mother could continue receiving assistance and working full time until she received the promotions necessary to support her family or could save up to launch a small business? "Cracking down" on welfare eligibility means that she is further incentivized to stay out of the workforce or make long-term financial plans.

Workers with Disabilities

Low-income families with children are not the only ones to feel trapped in poverty by counterproductive assistance rules. As the demand for low-skill labor has declined in recent decades, the number of people receiving disability payments has increased dramatically (Autor & Duggan, 2003; Joffe-Walt, n.d.-b). Supplemental Security Income (SSI) had 8.2 million recipients in 2018 (Center on Budget and Policy Priorities, 2018a) and Social Security Disability Insurance (SSDI; for recipients with sufficient work histories) had 8.6 million (Center on Budget and Policy Priorities, 2018b), compared to just 2.3 million individuals (or 1 million households) receiving TANF in the same year (Administration for Children and Families, 2018). Some economists have discovered that the mere availability of SSI and SSDI discourages work (Chen & van der Klaauw, 2008). Politicians might interpret these findings to mean that disability insurance must be made even more restrictive. However, the already low eligibility criteria to receive disability ($750 monthly income limit for individuals and $1125 for couples in SSI and $1180 per month in SSDI) (Center on Budget and Policy Priorities, 2018a, 2018b) may be the actual disincentive. In an era when living wage jobs are disappearing, why would a disabled worker jeopardize reliable disability income to take a riskier financial move such as a part-time job or starting a small business? Or, as one MTurker with disabilities explained, "there are a large number of rules that make it almost impossible to get ahead." I spoke to a former recipient of disability insurance who struggled with mental health concerns in Ontario, Canada, which has a similar income-restricted disability program to the United States. He explained to me that he wanted to be employed, but the nature of his disability made it difficult to maintain a job. "I don't know until I wake up if I'm going to have a good day or a bad day. Or a good week or a bad week. A good month or a bad month" (Hamilton & Mulvale, 2019, p. 592). For him, the risk of being fired from his job when he was having a bad week or a bad month was not worth losing more reliable income from the disability program, so he resigned himself not to pursue a job.

The passage of the Americans with Disability Act in 1990 was intended to integrate persons with disabilities into public life more successfully, but employment rates for this population have declined since its passage (Burkhauser & Daly, 2012). The ADA itself does not appear to be to blame, but the concomitant increase in SSI and SSDI beneficiaries and the trap this creates for workers with disabilities has played a significant role. While aging Baby Boomers account for about 6% of rising disability rolls (because you are more likely to become disabled as you get older), changes to the disability insurance caseload can be largely explained by new eligibility rules that allow more workers to receive benefits (Burkhauser & Daly, 2012). Once people receive disability, they are unlikely to return to work. In the ten years after a beneficiary begins receiving SSI or SSDI, they are more likely to remain on the program, die, or reach retirement age than return to work (Anand & Ben-Shalom, 2018).

Because TANF is funded by diminishing state block grants while the federal government funds disability insurance without budget limitations, states are incentivized to move low-income families from TANF to SSI. There is some evidence that states are actively doing just that (Joffe-Walt, n.d.-a); increased SSI receipt is significantly correlated with declining TANF caseloads. This program shift has been especially true in areas such as Appalachia where jobs in coal and manufacturing have all but disappeared (Wong, 2016). Finally, some SSI participants may be encouraged to apply because it also makes them eligible for Medicaid. When Medicaid was expanded under the Affordable Care Act, SSI rolls declined by 7% among childless adults (Burns & Dague, 2017).

Basic Income and Work

In the context of conditional welfare's well-established barriers to gainful employment, it is ironic that one of the primary objections to replacing it with a unconditional basic income is the belief that it would remove the incentive to work. When asked what people would do with a basic income, most people say that they would continue working. When asked what they think *other* people would do with a basic income, most believe that people would stop working (Standing, 2017). However, among the various basic income experiments around the world, the effects on labor are either small or not statistically significant (Gilbert, Murphy, Stepka, Barrett, & Worku, 2018; Marinescu, 2017).

In 2018, Gilbert and his colleagues (2018) published a review of 16 basic income trials across 12 countries, including five in the United States and one in Canada, spanning from the 1970s to a handful that are currently underway. The experiments included as few as 398 individuals in Namibia to 11 million people in Brazil's Bolsa Familia cash transfer program, which continues today. The amount of the cash transfers across the 16 studies ranges from a high of 18% of the country's household GDP in the 1970s Gary, Indiana trial to just 96 shillings in Uganda, which represents less than 1% of Uganda's household GDP.

The researchers looked at the total number of hours worked by recipients of basic income and the overall labor force participation rate (LPR). LPR is measured by dividing the number of working adults by the total number of adults who are eligible to work (not in an institution like prison and not in the military). Across the 16 studies, there were no significant changes to hours worked or the LPR before and after households began receiving a basic income. Interestingly, in some developing countries, work actually increased. The authors hypothesize that basic income allowed recipients to expand their work opportunities through investing in small businesses, buying equipment for farming, et cetera.

Some 1970s experiments in the United States and Canada did discover small decreases to work participation rates, primarily among women. Researchers hypothesized that basic income gave women more flexibility to care for young children (Marinescu, 2017). Because many of these experiments occurred in the late 1960s and early 1970s, it seems likely that many families would make different labor force and child care choices today since many more women have entered the workforce in the past 50 years. Qualitative interviews with Mincome recipients in 1976 revealed that some of the primary reasons they signed up for the experiment were to provide their family with a little extra security when work was unreliable or unavailable, or if they were ill, elderly, or disabled, or to enable further education. Only women with small children appeared to be motivated by the desire to work less, presumably in order to be primary caregivers (Calnitsky, 2016).

Several of the basic income recipients I spoke to in the modern Ontario pilot reported that their previous experiences with traditional Canadian welfare programs (which are not drastically different from those in America) discouraged work while basic income allowed them to pursue new opportunities without the threat of financial insecurity. One recipient told me about her experiences trying to get a job and work herself off of traditional welfare (Hamilton & Mulvale, 2019, p. 592).

> Almost everything seemed to interfere with any progress to gain work. So, I actually own a car, and I was allowed to keep the car but there was absolutely no money to keep a car on the road or insured. So the insurance [was] lost and yeah. I actually had a job offer at the time that I lost my car and because I have mobility issues—I don't walk well anymore—it was kind of "Can I take that job?" half of the income I would get from a part-time professional job would be taken back, still couldn't change my living circumstance which was living in a terrible rooming house. It's constantly, you cannot change your circumstances, you can get work—you can get all kinds of work but you can't change your living circumstance because half of it is taken back. That half that you keep goes to supporting what it takes to get there and the things that will allow you to keep the job…The social welfare system—every time I got a step ahead it would slam me back down.

Other recipients told me that they were returning to college or starting small businesses with basic income, ventures that were too risky under traditional welfare programs. The broader survey with over 400 Ontario recipients supports this finding, 32.46% of whom reported that they had returned to school to improve their long-term job prospects and 8.96% were able to launch or expand a small business (Basic Income Canada Network, 2019). Several participants further explained how basic income had allowed them to continue working or find work.

- "I could afford a proper home for our newborn baby and be able to provide for her while working a 50 hour a week full-time job."
- "I could afford transportation to work."
- "I was saving for a vehicle so I could pursue self-employment without fear of not making ends meet."
- "It helped fill in the gaps when I had precarious (part-time) employment while looking for something more sustainable."

Another common argument for basic income is that it allows people the flexibility to pursue more fulfilling but financially risky work, such as in the arts or non-profit sector. It can also empower people to take unpaid internships that create greater prospects in the long term but involve short-term financial precarity. Too many people are currently stuck in dead-end or unfulfilling work simply because they cannot risk the loss of economic security for themselves and their families. Several Ontario recipients reflected this experience (Basic Income Canada Network, 2019).

- "Even with a low employment income, I became more committed to my job serving a vulnerable population because I knew the basic income supplement would allow me to pay all of my bills and eat well."
- "I was able to search for a good apprenticeship without settling for something less professional."
- "It allowed me to start planning for the exhibition of my artwork."
- "I was choosing between two jobs; [I] was able to choose the one which paid less but was more fulfilling and more valuable professionally."

While welfare conditionality is associated with poorer health and lost economic productivity, in several basic income pilots, recipients reported improved mental and physical health. For example, unconditional casino dividends to Cherokee families with children who were very young when they began receiving stipends were less likely to have psychiatric disorders than children who were older (because the younger children would have had more years growing up without financial strain) (Yoshikawa, Aber, & Beardslee, 2012). In the 1970s Manitoba experiment, community-wide psychiatric hospitalization rates decreased by 8% (Forget, 2011), and in the modern Ontario pilot, more than 88% of participants reported reductions in stress and anxiety. Nearly 73% reported reductions in depression (Basic Income Canada Network, 2019).

Similarly, all of the Ontario basic income recipients I spoke with expressed that no longer relying on a meager and conditional income had tremendous positive effects on their mental health. One told me that "I like having a full fridge, I like living with dignity, and those are things you forget when you live in poverty and your daily thing is just surviving for the day." Another described basic income as not feeling "like I'm under a dark cloud and afraid to live." By comparison, this recipient described her experiences with traditional Canadian assistance thus.

> Every time I turn around; someone's looking over my shoulder, going to the bank every month thinking "Oh God, am I going to have money in there to pay the rent, buy some milk," whatever I need. [On basic income], I don't have to feel stress about that. (Hamilton & Mulvale, 2019)

Recipients in the modern Ontario pilot reported significant reductions in "migraines, fatigue, and depression [...] fibromyalgia, celiac disease or IBS. People succeeded in gaining or losing weight to be healthier. Some were also better able to manage other conditions or disabilities" (Basic Income Canada Network, 2019). Nearly a third were able to access dental care that they had previously put off, almost 45% had fewer health problems than when the pilot began, and 17% were able to reduce the use of medication through overall improvements to their health. One recipient, through improved access to health care and medication, was able to gain control of a chronic health condition, which "greatly reduced my stress, anxiety, depression" (Basic Income Canada Network, 2019).

Many of these improvements to the health of recipients were ascribed to improved nutrition. Nearly three quarters reported that they were able to make better food choices and almost a third stopped accessing food bank services. One respondent stated that "We were able to change the way [our daughter] ate...in order to live a normal life. She has since blossomed and overcame depression and anxiety with the proper foods she is getting...such a blessing to our family" (Basic Income Canada Network, 2019).

It's also important to consider the larger impact: A community-wide basic income pilot in Namibia discovered increased economic activity because people suddenly had money to spend, which in turn led to small business growth and increased employment. Overall, average income rose beyond the amount of cash transfers (Haarmann et al., 2008). The Roosevelt Institute estimates that basic income would have a similar effect on the US economy. In their projections, giving every adult $1000 per month would expand the economy by 12.56% over eight years (Nikiforos, Steinbaum, & Zezza, 2017), by creating new demand for goods and resultantly, new jobs.

In an era when the global economy continues to pressure businesses to increase profits and decrease costs, basic income should be seen as a supplement to employers to remain competitive in the global market rather than a deterrent to work. With an unconditional basic income, workers would be free to take on part-time, low-wage, non-profit, or "gig" work, without fear of jeopardizing their fundamental financial security as they currently are under traditional welfare programs. Among low-wage workers, 40% already experience significant income volatility, in which their household income spikes or drops by at least 25%, six or more times per year (Maag, Peters, Hannagan, Lou, & Siwicki, 2017), making these workers hypothetically but only intermittently eligible for benefits. One MTurker and former recipient of Unemployment Insurance explained that the program "discouraged me from taking temporary work."

Further, we could end the use of expensive and ineffective "welfare to work" programs, which primarily seem to punish the poor for economic conditions outside their control and allow politicians to say that they are cracking down on "dependence." As one basic income recipient in Ontario explained, the pilot…

> allowed us to make future long term plans that were attainable…[I'm] tired of lies and being cheated so wealthy people can get wealthier. I have worked my whole life and never seem to get anywhere; the system has been broken a long time. (Basic Income Canada Network, 2019)

References

Abramovitz, M. (1996). *Regulating the Lives of Women: Social Welfare Policy from Colonial Times to the Present.* Boston: South End Press.

Abramovitz, M. (2006). Neither Accidental, Nor Simply Mean-Spirited: The Context for Welfare Reform. In K. Kilty & E. Segal (Eds.), *The Promise of Welfare Reform: Political Rhetoric and Reality of Poverty in the Twenty-First Century* (pp. 23–37). New York: Hawthorne.

Administration for Children and Families. (2018). *TANF Caseload Data 2018.* Retrieved March 22, 2019, from Office of Family Assistance | ACF Website: https://www.acf.hhs.gov/ofa/resource/tanf-caseload-data-2018

Ahn, H. (2012). Child Care Subsidy, Child Care Costs, and Employment of Low-Income Single Mothers. *Children and Youth Services Review, 34*(2), 379–387. https://doi.org/10.1016/j.childyouth.2011.11.010.

Anand, P., & Ben-Shalom, Y. (2018). Pathways Taken by New Social Security Disability Insurance and Supplemental Security Income Awardees. *Journal of Disability Policy Studies, 29*(3), 153–165. https://doi.org/10.1177/1044207318779987.

Autor, D., & Duggan, M. (2003). The Rise in the Disability Rolls and the Decline in Unemployment. *The Quarterly Journal of Economics, 1*, 157.

Basic Income Canada Network. (2019). *Signposts to Success: Report of a BICN Survey of Ontario Basic Income Recipients.* Retrieved from Basic Income Canada Network Website: https://www.basicincomecanada.org/time_for_national_action_new_report_shows_ontario_basic_income_pilot_was_on_track_to_success?fbclid=IwAR1BcwCr6pQ-kLHv_YRXddbK48jv2OLH9pGX-X1rU_946RB-Kvro2wvVrCg

Bitler, M. P., Gelbach, J. B., & Hoynes, H. W. (2005). Welfare Reform and Health. *Journal of Human Resources, XL*(2), 309–334. https://doi.org/10.3368/jhr.XL.2.309.

Black, R., & Sprague, A. (2017). *Becoming Visible: Race, Economic Security, and Political Voice in Jackson, Mississippi.* Retrieved from New America Foundation Website: https://www.newamerica.org/family-centered-social-policy/policy-papers/becoming-visible/

Blau, J. (2006). Welfare Reform in Historical Perspective. In K. Kilty & E. Segal (Eds.), *The Promise of Welfare Reform: Political Rhetoric and Reality of Poverty in the Twenty-First Century* (pp. 49–56). New York: Hawthorne.

Booker, B. (2018, December 20). *Trump Signs Farm Bill, Backs Rule Sidestepping Congress on More Work for Food Stamps.* Retrieved March 18, 2019, from NPR.org Website: https://www.npr.org/2018/12/20/678593200/sidestepping-congress-trump-administration-proposes-more-work-rules-for-food-sta

Brooks, F. P., Mack, S. E., Chaney, A. E., Gibson, K., & Caplan, M. (2018). TANF Leavers and Economic Self-Sufficiency: Results from a Study in Georgia. *Journal of Poverty, 22*(5), 454–470. https://doi.org/10.1080/10875549.2018.1460739.

Burkhauser, R., & Daly, M. (2012). Social Security Disability Insurance: Time for Fundamental Change. *Journal of Policy Analysis and Management, 31*(2), 454. https://doi.org/10.1002/pam.21618.

Burns, M., & Dague, L. (2017). The Effect of Expanding Medicaid Eligibility on Supplemental Security Income Program Participation. *Journal of Public Economics, 149*, 20–34. https://doi.org/10.1016/j.jpubeco.2017.03.004.

Calnitsky, D. (2016). "More Normal than Welfare": The Mincome Experiment, Stigma, and Community Experience. *Canadian Review of Sociology/Revue Canadienne de Sociologie, 53*(1), 26–71. https://doi.org/10.1111/cars.12091.

Center on Budget and Policy Priorities. (2015). *Policy Basics: An Introduction to TANF.* Retrieved July 19, 2017, from Center on Budget and Policy Priorities Website: https://www.cbpp.org/research/policy-basics-an-introduction-to-tanf

Center on Budget and Policy Priorities. (2018a). *Policy Basics: Social Security Disability Insurance.* Retrieved from Center on Budget and Policy Priorities

Website: https://www.cbpp.org/research/retirement-security/policy-basics-social-security-disability-insurance

Center on Budget and Policy Priorities. (2018b). *Policy Basics: Supplemental Security Income*. Retrieved March 21, 2019, from Center on Budget and Policy Priorities Website: https://www.cbpp.org/research/social-security/policy-basics-supplemental-security-income

Center on Budget and Policy Priorities. (2019, February 19). *Policy Brief: How States Use Funds Under the TANF Block Grant*. Retrieved March 15, 2019, from Center on Budget and Policy Priorities Website: https://www.cbpp.org/research/family-income-support/policy-brief-how-states-use-funds-under-the-tanf-block-grant

Centers for Disease Control. (2019, March 5). *Health and Economic Costs of Chronic Disease*. Retrieved from https://www.cdc.gov/chronicdisease/about/costs/index.htm

Chen, S., & van der Klaauw, W. (2008). The Work Disincentive Effects of the Disability Insurance Program in the 1990s. *Journal of Econometrics, 142*, 757–784. https://doi.org/10.1016/j.jeconom.2007.05.016.

Cheng, T. (2007). Impact of Work Requirements on the Psychological Well-Being of TANF Recipients. *Health & Social Work, 32*(1), 41–48.

Federal Reserve Board. (1997, July 22). *Testimony of Chairman Alan Greenspan*. Retrieved November 29, 2018, from The Federal Reserve's Semiannual Monetary Policy Report Website: https://www.federalreserve.gov/boarddocs/hh/1997/july/testimony.htm

Fording, R. C., Schram, S. F., & Soss, J. (2013). Do Welfare Sanctions Help or Hurt the Poor? Estimating the Causal Effect of Sanctioning on Client Earnings. *Social Service Review, 87*(4), 641–676. https://doi.org/10.1086/674111.

Forget, E. L. (2011). The Town with No Poverty: The Health Effects of a Canadian Guaranteed Annual Income Field Experiment. *Canadian Public Policy, 37*(3), 283–305. https://doi.org/10.3138/cpp.37.3.283.

Gilbert, R., Murphy, N. A., Stepka, A., Barrett, M., & Worku, D. (2018). Would a Basic Income Guarantee Reduce the Motivation to Work? An Analysis of Labor Responses in 16 Trial Programs. *Basic Income Studies, 13*(2). https://doi.org/10.1515/bis-2018-0011.

Gold, S. F. (1971). The Failure of the Work Incentive (WIN) Program. *University of Pennsylvania Law Review, 119*(3), 485–501. https://doi.org/10.2307/3311311.

Gross, C. L., Church, J., Taylor, T., & Towne-Roese, J. K. (2018). "Between a Rock and a Hard Place": The Constraints of Welfare-to-Work Bureaucracies. *Poverty & Public Policy, 10*(1), 39–56.

Haarmann, C., Haarmann, D., Jauch, H., Shindonola-Mote, H., Nattrass, N., Samson, M., & Standing, G. (2008). *Towards a Basic Income Grant for All: Basic Income Grant Pilot Project Assessment Report, September 2008*. Retrieved

from NANGOF Website: http://www.bignam.org/Publications/BIG_Assessment_report_08a.pdf
Hamilton, L., & Mulvale, J. P. (2019). "Human Again": The (Unrealized) Promise of Basic Income in Ontario. *Journal of Poverty, 23*(7), 576–599. https://doi.org/10.1080/10875549.2019.1616242.
Hildebrandt, E. (2016). Understanding the Lives and Challenges of Women in Poverty After TANF. *Policy, Politics, & Nursing Practice, 17*(3), 156–169. https://doi.org/10.1177/1527154416672204.
Joffe-Walt, C. (n.d.-a). *Trends with Benefits*. In *This American Life*. Retrieved from https://www.thisamericanlife.org/490/trends-with-benefits/act-two-0
Joffe-Walt, C. (n.d.-b). *Unfit for Work: The Startling Rise of Disability in America*. Retrieved March 21, 2019, from http://apps.npr.org/unfit-for-work/
Kim, J. (2018). The Timing of Exemptions from Welfare Work Requirements and Its Effect on Mother's Work and Welfare Receipt Around Childbirth. *Economic Inquiry, 56*(1), 317. Retrieved from Biography In Context.
Larbee, M. (1939). *Unmarried Parenthood Under the Social Security Act*. Presented at the National Conference of Social Work, New York.
Lim, Y., Coulton, C. J., & Lalich, N. (2009). State TANF Policies and Employment Outcomes Among Welfare Leavers. *Social Service Review, 83*(4), 525–555.
Lower-Basch, E. (2018). *Work Participation Rate: Temporary Assistance for Needy Families* (p. 8). Washington, DC: Center for Law and Social Policy.
Maag, E., Peters, H. E., Hannagan, A., Lou, C., & Siwicki, J. (2017). *Income Volatility: New Research Results with Implications for Income Tax Filing and Liabilities*. Retrieved from Tax Policy Center Website: https://www.taxpolicycenter.org/publications/income-volatility-new-research-results-implications-income-tax-filing-and-liabilities/full
Madill, R. (2017). *Why Millions of Eligible Children Miss Out on Federal Child Care Grants*. Retrieved from Child Trends Website: https://www.childtrends.org/millions-eligible-children-miss-federal-child-care-grants
Marinescu, I. (2017). *No Strings Attached: The Behavioral Effects of U.S. Unconditional Cash Transfer Programs*. Retrieved from Roosevelt Institute Website: http://rooseveltinstitute.org/wp-content/uploads/2017/05/No-Strings-Attached-050417-1.pdf
Marshall, N. L., Robeson, W. W., Tracy, A. J., Frye, A., & Roberts, J. (2013). Subsidized Child Care, Maternal Employment and Access to Quality, Affordable Child Care. *Early Childhood Research Quarterly, 28*(4), 808–819. https://doi.org/10.1016/j.ecresq.2013.07.008.
Minton, S., & Durham, C. (2013, December 23). *Low-Income Families and the Cost of Child Care: State Child Care Subsidies, Out-of-Pocket Expenses and the Cliff Effect [Text]*. Retrieved June 5, 2014, from http://www.urban.org/publications/412982.html

Monnat, S. M. (2010). The Color of Welfare Sanctioning: Exploring the Individual and Contextual Roles of Race on TANF Case Closures and Benefit Reductions. *The Sociological Quarterly, 51*(4), 678–707. https://doi.org/10.1111/j.1533-8525.2010.01188.x.

Nikiforos, M., Steinbaum, M., & Zezza, G. (2017). *Modeling the Macroeconomic Effects of a Universal Basic Income*. Retrieved from Roosevelt Institute Website: http://rooseveltinstitute.org/modeling-macroeconomic-effects-ubi/

Pew Charitable Trusts. (2016). *Child Care Subsidies, Vital for Many Workers, Are Dwindling*. Retrieved from Pew Charitable Trusts Website: http://pew.org/2gpl8zi

Piven, F. F., & Cloward, R. (1993). *Regulating the Poor: The Functions of Public Welfare* (Updated, Subsequent ed.). New York: Vintage.

Roll, S., & East, J. (2014). Financially Vulnerable Families and the Child Care Cliff Effect. *Journal of Poverty, 18*(2), 169–187. https://doi.org/10.1080/10875549.2014.896307.

Schram, S. F. (2006). That Old Black Magic? Welfare Reform and the New Politics of Racial Implication. In K. Kilty & E. Segal (Eds.), *The Promise of Welfare Reform: Political Rhetoric and Reality of Poverty in the Twenty-First Century* (pp. 223–235). New York: Hawthorne.

Seccombe, K., Walters, K. B., & James, D. (1999). "Welfare Mothers" Welcome Reform, Urge Compassion. *Family Relations, 48*(2), 197–206. https://doi.org/10.2307/585084.

Seefeldt, K. S. (2017). Serving No One Well: TANF Nearly Twenty Years Later. *Journal of Sociology & Social Welfare, 44*(2), 3–28.

Shapiro, T. M. (2017). *Toxic Inequality: How America's Wealth Gap Destroys Mobility, Deepens the Racial Divide, and Threatens Our Future*. New York: Basic Books.

Sieh, E. W. (1989). Less Eligibility: The Upper Limits of Penal Policy. *Criminal Justice Policy Review, 3*(2), 159–183. https://doi.org/10.1177/088740348900300204.

Standing, G. (2017). *Basic Income: A Guide for the Open-Minded*. New Haven, CT/London: Yale University Press.

Stiglitz, J. E. (2012). *The Price of Inequality: How Today's Divided Society Endangers Our Future* (1st ed.). New York: W. W. Norton & Company.

Taylor, T., Gross, C. L., & Towne-Roese, J. K. (2016). Program Barriers and Challenges to Self-Sufficiency: A Qualitative Analysis of Ohio Welfare-to-Work Program Manager Identity. *Critical Sociology, 42*(7–8), 1125–1141. https://doi.org/10.1177/0896920515569084.

Wong, S. (2016). Geographies of Medicalized Welfare: Spatial Analysis of Supplemental Security Income in the U.S., 2000–2010. *Social Science & Medicine, 160*, 9–19. https://doi.org/10.1016/j.socscimed.2016.05.018.

World Health Organization. (2009). *Economic Burden of Disease*. Retrieved from World Health Organization Website: http://www.who.int/choice/economicburden/en/

Wu, C.-F., Cancian, M., & Wallace, G. (2014). The Effect of Welfare Sanctions on TANF Exits and Employment. *Children and Youth Services Review, 36*, 1–14. https://doi.org/10.1016/j.childyouth.2013.10.022.

Ybarra, M., & Noyes, J. L. (2019). Program and Economic Outcomes by TANF Work Exemption Status. *Journal of the Society for Social Work and Research, 10*(1), 97–125. https://doi.org/10.1086/702408.

Yoshikawa, H., Aber, L., & Beardslee, W. (2012). The Effects of Poverty on the Mental, Emotional, and Behavioral Health of Children and Youth: Implications for Prevention. *American Psychologist, 67*(4), 272–284.

Zedlewski, S. R. (2016). *Welfare Reform What Have We Learned in Fifteen Years?* Retrieved from Urban Institute Website: https://www.urban.org/research/publication/welfare-reform-what-have-we-learned-fifteen-years

CHAPTER 3

Perverse Incentives

Abstract Modern social policy is heavily influenced by "culture of poverty" theory, paternalism, and stereotypes about welfare recipients which are unsupported by research. Attempts to shape the behavior of those living in poverty through intrusive welfare eligibility criteria has frequently been ineffective and sometimes detrimental. Meanwhile, basic income pilots reveal decreases in crime and other negative social behaviors. Understanding the effects of financial scarcity and trusting all people to make their own life choices is arguably a more effective and humane basis for social policy design.

Keywords Behavior • Paternalism • Scarcity • Incentives

Paternalism and Social Policy

Concerns about welfare don't stop at the effects to work. Our current poverty alleviation programs are heavily influenced by a dominant "culture of poverty" theory, championed by writers like Charles Murray (2008), which posits that specific negative characteristics or behaviors are passed generationally between families in poverty. This theory argues that some personality flaw among the poor makes assistance a waste of resources, and to truly remediate poverty, we must control the behavior of the poor.

Arguably, these ideas are not significantly different from the theories of Social Darwinism and Eugenics, which dominated social policy design in the late 1800s and early 1900s. Taking Charles Darwin's theory of

L. Hamilton, *Welfare Doesn't Work*, Exploring the Basic Income Guarantee, https://doi.org/10.1007/978-3-030-37121-0_3

evolution to the extreme, Social Darwinists believed that wealth was a signal of genetic superiority and poverty was therefore indicative of genetic defect. The only solution was to prevent the poor from reproducing. Proponents of Eugenics in the United States and Europe argued that the "feebleminded," those with mental illness, disabilities, and disproportionately, low-income minorities, ought to be forcibly sterilized to prevent them from having children and passing on undesirable traits. This school of thought inspired many of the Nazi Party's most heinous acts in World War II (Farber, 2008). More than 60,000 Americans were involuntarily sterilized until the practice ended in the 1970s (Minna Stern, 2016). In the 1950s, state Eugenics Boards—as they were called—began applying the philosophy to poor women and their daughters as a method of preventing generational "dependence," with some states attempting to make sterilization a requirement of receiving welfare (Pierson-Balik, 2003). In North Carolina, for example, a 12-year-old was sterilized because she was "often away from home" and "constantly talk[ed] about boyfriends" (Rose, n.d.).

We now look at the Eugenics movement as a shameful chapter in our country's history. But the idea that the poor are inherently inferior human beings and need intervention to prevent negative intergenerational behavioral patterns has not entirely disappeared from social policy rhetoric. The culture of poverty theory propels several harmful myths, including the idea that most welfare recipients are black, Hispanic, or even undocumented immigrants, are lazy and just need to get a job, are more likely to use drugs, trade their Food Stamps/SNAP for drugs, alcohol, and cigarettes, remain on the program for years, and intentionally have more children to get additional benefits. Let's look at these myths one by one.

Are Most Welfare Recipients Black, Latinx, or Immigrants?

The simple answer to this question is a resounding "no." Minority families *do* represent a higher proportion of public assistance recipients than they do in the general population, but that is because structural discrimination causes people of color to be statistically overrepresented in poverty. Still, less than one in three adult TANF recipients were black in 2017 and 30.4% were Latino. White households made up most of the remaining third, along with small percentages of Native American, Asian, and multiracial families (Administration for Children and Families, 2018). In the SNAP program, 35.8% of recipients are white, 25.4% are black, and 16.5% are

Hispanic (Cronquist & Lauffer, 2019). When aggregating all means-tested assistance programs (housing assistance, Medicaid, SNAP, SSI, TANF, and other short-term cash assistance programs), African Americans make up less than 25% of beneficiaries (Foster & Rojas, 2018).

The idea that immigrants, and especially undocumented immigrants, come to the United States to access our social service system is both blanketly untrue and dangerous to the political viability of the safety net. The Personal Responsibility and Work Opportunity Reconciliation Act of 1996 barred all legal immigrants from TANF, SNAP, Medicaid, and the Children's Health Insurance Program (CHIP) for their first five years in the country. Undocumented immigrants are banned from *all* programs (US Department of Health and Human Services, 2012).

Do Welfare Recipients Work?

A study at the University of California, Berkeley examined nationwide recipients of TANF, SNAP, the Earned Income Tax Credit (EITC), Medicaid, and CHIP. Almost three quarters (73%) of recipients in these programs have at least one member who works at least part-time (Jacobs, Perry, & MacGillvary, 2015). The three most common jobs for recipients are fast food workers, child-care workers, and home health aides. Of *all* workers in these three fields, roughly half receive some form of public assistance. The fourth most common category was part-time college faculty, 25% of whom receive assistance. As discussed in Chap. 2, public welfare is not a subsidy to laziness; it is a subsidy to low-wage employers and a declining median wage. The researchers estimated that employers who do not pay a living wage cost taxpayers $152.8 billion per year in welfare expenditures (Jacobs et al., 2015).

Do Welfare Recipients Use More Drugs?

There's a widespread belief that beneficiaries of public assistance use drugs more frequently than the general population and their welfare benefits are being spent on illegal substances. Fifteen states have now enacted drug testing for public assistance, and at least 20 other state legislatures have considered it. This idea continues to percolate in public discourse despite a lack of credible evidence to support it.

In Florida, after implementing drug testing for TANF, only 2.6% of recipients were positive. By comparison, an estimated 6% of all Floridians use drugs (Lyle, 2012). In the 2014 National Survey on Drug Use and Health, less than 15% of TANF recipients had used an illicit drug other than marijuana in the past year (Oh, DiNitto, & Kim, 2018). In Florida's drug testing scheme, applicants paid $30–$35 for the test but were reimbursed if the test was negative. Overall, drug testing cost the state over $100,000 because reimbursements totaled more than was saved in denied welfare benefits (Dallas News, 2013). This also creates an undue burden on applicants. Thirty-five dollars is a significant amount of money if you are already experiencing financial precarity. Similarly in Utah, between August 2012 and August 2013, only 12 applicants tested positive, with a net cost to the state of $25,000 (Price, 2013).

After 4 months of drug testing TANF applicants in Florida, a judge ruled the policy unconstitutional because it violated an applicant's rights against unlawful search and seizure. The Fourth Amendment of the US Constitution states that:

> The right of the people to be secure in their persons, houses, papers, and effects, against unreasonable searches and seizures, shall not be violated, and no warrants shall issue, but upon probable cause, supported by oath or affirmation, and particularly describing the place to be searched, and the persons or things to be seized.

In other words, unless a person is suspected of a crime and the police have a warrant or probable cause, they cannot search a person's belongings or their body. This protection should extend, in the judge's argument, to welfare recipients because a very low income is not sufficient to suspect a person of using drugs.

Furthermore, what if a parent *is* struggling with addiction? Shall we deny their children basic security? Instead of removing assistance to parents who test positive, we could instead offer rehabilitation services while ensuring that the family still has food and shelter. It is difficult to fight addiction when you are otherwise distracted by homelessness, food insecurity, or the threat of losing your children to foster care. One of the most powerful experiences of my social work education was touring a women's drug treatment facility that included housing for those in recovery *and* their children. Multiple studies have confirmed that inpatient treatment which includes children improves the likelihood of a mother's recovery (Center for Substance Abuse Treatment, 2009). Unfortunately, these services are often few and far between (Jackson, 2004). Long wait lists mean that children enter the foster care system or are even adopted before their mothers receive treatment (Rockhill, Green, & Newton-Curtis, 2007).

Do Welfare Recipients Misuse Their Funds?

Culture of poverty theories further perpetuate the belief that SNAP recipients fraudulently sell benefits in exchange for drugs, alcohol, or cigarettes. When I teach social policy to undergraduates, there's usually one student with a story (that they heard from someone, who heard from someone else) that Food Stamps were being trafficked outside their local gas station. These anecdotes aside, the fraud rate in SNAP is estimated by the Congressional Research Service to be 1.5% (Aussenberg, 2018). Moreover, when fraud does occur, the criminals are prosecuted. By comparison, the estimated Medicare fraud rate is approximately 8% (US Government Accountability Office, 2019), but I have yet to hear calls to terminate healthcare for seniors to prevent program misuse.

Do Welfare Recipients Remain on Assistance Long Term?

The notion that people in poverty remain on assistance for long periods of time is outdated. With five-year lifetime limits (and 24 months in any one stint) implemented in 1996, it is practically impossible for recipients to stay on assistance long term unless they receive a special hardship waiver. In 2017, only 7.2% of all TANF cases had received such an exemption. Most (57.5%) of the 517,722 active TANF households in 2017 had been receiving assistance for less than 24 months (Administration for Children and Families, 2018).

While qualitative research with TANF recipients reveals that they too disapprove of long-term dependence, one mother explained that "sometimes it takes people a little longer than that [24 months] to get on their feet" (Seccombe, Walters, & James, 1999, p. 200). Eight in ten TANF recipients face at least one significant barrier to employment (poor mental or physical health, lack of an HS diploma, limited work experience, care of a disabled family member, or fleeing domestic violence) and more than 40% face two to three barriers (Bloom, Loprest, & Zedlewski, 2012). One TANF recipient felt strongly that time limits reflected ignorance of the complexity of recipients' lives (Seccombe et al., 1999, p. 201).

> How can you put a timeline on someone's life? I see what they are trying to do. They are trying to get those individuals who they feel aren't making efforts off the rolls. But I don't agree with that. Setting an arbitrary time limit on a system that is so dysfunctional to begin with that, you know, it's amazing that anyone gets off it…It's very easy up in Washington to sit on their thrones, as it were, and to say 'Oh, they're lazy' and this and that. But it doesn't hit home until you are in this situation. I think it would do them good to go and visit these people themselves.

Do Recipients Have Additional Children So They Can Get More Welfare?

Finally, there's a belief that some mothers become pregnant with the express intention of getting additional assistance. Even in interviews with TANF mothers themselves, they too believed this myth, while none personally knew anyone who had done this (Seccombe et al., 1999). Harkening to the Eugenics movement and its application to welfare recipients in the 1950s and '60s, several states offered cash incentives to welfare mothers for receiving Norplant devices (long-term birth control) well into the 1990s. South Carolina and Mississippi even considered making it a requirement of TANF receipt (Pierson-Balik, 2003). More recently, family caps, currently implemented in 14 states (Urban Institute, 2018), limit assistance when a family has additional children while receiving TANF. Essentially, this means that even though TANF payments are usually based on household size, if you have a baby while receiving assistance, your grant doesn't get adjusted upwards to account for the additional child.

Here again, these beliefs are not supported by existent data. The average size of TANF households is 2.5 people (including adults) and more than half of all TANF households have only one child (Falk, 2016), compared to 2.4 children in the average American family (Livingston, 2015). Linda Tirado (an author, mother, and former welfare recipient) refuted this belief in her popular book, *Hand to Mouth: Living in Bootstrap America* (Tirado, 2015) by arguing that having more children in order to get additional welfare is akin to intentionally injuring yourself to get free meals at the hospital. More to the point, when asked about family caps, one TANF mother asked researchers, "Who would have a baby just for fifty bucks a month" (Seccombe et al., 1999, p. 203)?

Welfare and Behavioral Incentives

The belief that people with low income are inherently flawed human beings and require more supervision than people in middle- and upper-income households has been profoundly influential in social policy. Multiple current policies seek to shape behavior among welfare recipients including promoting marriage, decreasing birth rates, and enforcing paternal involvement via child support. The most common method of "incentivizing" these behaviors is through financial sanctions. In 2016, I published an article in which I reviewed the current body of literature examining incentives in the TANF program (Hamilton, 2016). I reviewed three academic search engines[1] for every article written since 1996 that included the words "incentive" and "Temporary Assistance to Needy Families." Commonalities among the relevant articles coalesced across the dimensions of work, family, and economic self-sufficiency. As discussed extensively in Chap. 2, research in the area of TANF and employment incentives generally finds that harsh work requirements are ultimately counterproductive and discourage employment.

In the family sphere, TANF efforts to enforce social norms for family formation have usually been either unsuccessful or even harmful. For example, the PRWORA of 1996 sought to encourage marriage since married couples, on average, have higher incomes and therefore need less public assistance. Even before 1996, several states experimented with "waivers," which implemented some of the dominant features of TANF including "work requirements, financial sanctions, time limits, liberalized earnings disregards (lower tax rates on earned income while on welfare), increased limits on financial assets, and expanded eligibility for two-parent families" (Bitler, Gelbach, Hoynes, & Zavodny, 2004, p. 216). Eligibility for two-parent families could hypothetically increase marriage rates, but the effects of other features are debatable. Would time limits and work requirements make welfare dependence less attractive and incentivize marriage? Or would the mental strain of these requirements squash romance?

Bitler and colleagues (2004) took advantage of these various policy changes to examine state by state marriage rates between 1989 and 2000. They controlled for other state-level demographics that might influence marriage rates such as unemployment, median income, age, race, and education. The researchers found that restrictions in TANF and pre-1996

[1] Academic One File, JSTOR, and Academic Search Complete.

TANF-like waivers decreased marriage rates at a statistically significant level. The authors hypothesize that work requirements made single mothers more independent and less likely to choose marriage for financial security. A similar study found that TANF use was associated with decreased marriage rates, but had no influence on cohabitation (Cherlin & Fomby, 2004), suggesting that TANF made marriage an economic calculation more than a personal one. In other words, despite TANF's stated intention of increasing two-parent families, strict eligibility criteria have had the opposite effect.

Other noteworthy effects (or lack thereof) to family formation are seen in the areas of family caps, teen parenting, and child support enforcement. Caps on assistance for children born after a family is already receiving TANF have had little effect on birth rates (Kearney, 2004; Wallace, 2009), although requiring teen parent recipients to live with a guardian and attend school has reduced the rate of subsequent births (Lopoo & DeLeire, 2006). Finally, "while some state TANF agencies retain child support payments for administrative costs, those passing the payments on to the mother and child experience faster paternity establishment and higher rates of payment" (Cancian, Meyer, & Caspar, 2008; Hamilton, 2016, p. 145).

Not all of the attempts to shape participant behavior have been merely pointless or a waste of resources. Some have been outright harmful, especially to children. Welfare sanctions are associated with poorer school performance (Larson, Singh, & Lewis, 2011) because when children do not have access to food and basic security, it is difficult to concentrate in school. Further, the implementation of TANF and subsequent caseload decline has increased family strain (because poverty is stressful), child abuse (because parenting suffers when one is under stress), and foster care placements (Swann & Sylvester, 2006).

Finally, of the studies that examined incentives for economic independence in the TANF program, most found that restrictive TANF criteria didn't create more self-sufficiency among families. Instead, onerous application processes deterred needy families from even applying (Ridzi & London, 2006) and pushed them to other programs like SNAP (Cancian, Meyer, & Wu, 2005; Hamilton, 2016). The failure of these attempts to influence the personal choices of the poor indicates an inadequate understanding of the complexity of human experience and the disastrous consequences of denying even small amounts of assistance to families in extreme need.

Poverty and Human Behavior

Of course, this discussion is not meant to imply that people living in poverty never make self-defeating choices. It is well documented that people with low incomes can make suboptimal financial and personal decisions (Mani, Mullainathan, Shafir, & Zhao, 2013). However, our previous efforts to incentivize and change the behavior of this population have either failed or exacerbated the issue because they have overlooked the psychological effects of "scarcity." Sendhil Mullainathan and Eldar Shafir released a revealing book on the subject in 2013 that looked at the impacts of living with not enough, based on a new area of research, behavioral economics (Mullainathan & Shafir, 2013). Economists have classically assumed that people make rational, self-optimizing choices, but commonsense tells us that this is not always the case.

Mullainathan and Shafir (2013) argue that when a resource is scarce, whether it is money, time, or interestingly, calories in the case of dieters, people tend to make poor choices with their remaining resources. Their brain "tunnels" on the scarce resource and it becomes unable to think about the bigger picture. They argue that humans have limited "mental bandwidth" and that "tunneling" on a pressing issue, like day to day financial survival, can limit our ability to think about other things. As an example, in one study, some classrooms in a particular school faced a railroad track where noisy trains would go by several times a day. This distraction was taxing to the student's mental bandwidth and put those nearest the train a full year behind their peers academically, even though they were demographically similar.

Similar effects were found on the mental bandwidth of survey respondents who were poor and asked to think about their finances before completing logic and IQ tests. Poor respondents fared significantly worse on these tests after they were prompted to think about a pressing financial issue in their current life. Further, mental bandwidth interference spills over into rational decision-making processes and even impulse control. Mullainathan and Shafir believe that this explains why some in poverty struggle to manage the necessary skills for economic self-sufficiency. A TANF program manager in a separate study expressed similar concerns that TANF recipients often struggle with basic life management skills such as punctuality and dependability in employment settings (Taylor, Gross, & Towne-Roese, 2016).

To illustrate the psychological effects of scarcity, I often show a Ted Talk by Eldar Shafir in my university courses (TEDx Talks, 2011). Shafir explains the basic concepts of scarcity and how it can apply to both money and time. Afterward, I ask students, "Have you ever had a looming deadline—say for a class paper—and not used your scarce time optimally? For example, binging on Netflix or other unproductive activities?" Invariably, I see a room full of sheepish smiles and knowing nods.

Still, how do we separate the culture of poverty theory with the theory of scarcity? Both work from the assumption that people in poverty make self-destructive decisions. However, while the culture of poverty theory says there is something specifically wrong with the personal character of people living in poverty, scarcity says that *everyone* acts differently when they are short on time, money, or other resources. In other words, poverty leads to bad choices rather than bad choices causing poverty.

A Cure for Bad Choices?

When I first became a social worker, I chose to work with children because, while I was skeptical of some adults, I knew that children were innocent and genuinely deserving of help. The children on my caseload suffered unspeakable abuse and neglect. These traumas resulted in significant effects on the children's physical, mental, and emotional health. Often, the children would be so wounded from these experiences, that they would lash out toward their foster parents, foster siblings, and even pets. Some children would have uncontrollable rages—screaming, kicking, hitting—for hours and the only advice we could give foster parents in the moment was to remove any sharp objects and get out of the way. As these children became teens, while their peers were taking college preparatory courses and driver's education, learning how to open a bank account, and write a check, many on my caseload were utterly preoccupied with making sense of their lives, often in ways destructive to themselves or others. Then, eventually, they turned 18. One day, they hold the world's sympathy, and the next day, none. They are suddenly expected to be an adult, get a job, pay rent, and generally be good citizens. Someday, they might become parents, and the cycle begins anew.

When I was an undergraduate social work intern, I went with my supervisor to the hospital to help with the discharge of a five-month-old baby who was going into foster care. The baby had been shaken so severely that his skull was fractured and his retinas detached. Though he was lucky to be alive, the doctor explained that he would likely have brain damage and be blind for the rest of his life. Just looking at that baby was one of the hardest things I have done in my career. His eyes were unfocused; he must have been in incredible pain that he could not articulate, and you could see a ridge across the top of his scalp where his skull was fractured. While my supervisor and the foster parents talked to the doctors and nurses about how to care for a baby with such extreme needs, it somehow fell to me to dress the baby. I was terrified of causing him any more pain. I very gently slipped a little onesie and pants on; so slowly, so carefully. But then, when it was time to put on the tiny knit cap, I could not do it. I tried a few times to get the hat over his uneven scalp, but my hands were shaking with fear of hurting him or causing more damage. That little boy will grow up needing significant support to build a life with his probable disabilities, and he will hold the world's sympathy, until the day he turns 18 and his brain damage affects his impulse control, he has difficulty maintaining employment, or he lashes out at someone else.

A few years later, after I graduated, two teenage sisters on my caseload had IQs just low enough to qualify them as having developmental disabilities. They were otherwise normal teenage girls who wanted to live normal teenage girls' lives, or at least as they saw them. Their mother also had a developmental disability and worked a simple job at a fast food restaurant; while their father was of average intelligence. The couple met when the mother was 18, and the father was in his late thirties. Because of the age and intellectual differences between their parents, all their lives, the girls observed their mother almost totally dependent upon their father for decision making, safety, and financial security. This is how the girls thought all male and female relationships work.

It was not surprising then that the girls were desperate for the same kind of security. They talked nonstop about getting boyfriends; no matter how hard I idealistically tried to explain that they could be strong, independent women. Their desperation for boyfriends was apparent when they went to school and boys easily took advantage of them. I was called multiple times into meetings because the girls had been performing oral sex in the bathroom on any boy who showed them the least bit of attention. I was only their caseworker for about a year, so I don't know what happened to the sisters. But, without significant intervention, I imagined it was only a matter of time until one or both of them became pregnant. Then, they would turn 18 and be young mothers with no idea how to function in the world, let alone how to parent effectively. And yet, they would be living in a world that tells them to stand on their own feet, get a job, and show some personal responsibility.

These cases are not anomalies. Less than 3% of former foster youth earn a college degree by age 25, only 9% have their own residence at age 26, 68% of males and 42% of females will be arrested by age 26, and 71% of females emancipating from foster care will be pregnant by age 21 (Fryar, Jordan, & Devooght, 2017). Of course, not every person who commits a crime or has a drug addiction was a foster child, but my experiences as a social worker have helped me to understand that many, many people are carrying unspeakable traumas in their lives that do not magically disappear upon adulthood. They also will not magically disappear if given an unconditional $12,000 per year. But, it is much easier to focus on attending therapy or drug treatment or returning for a GED if you have a roof over your head and food in your stomach. A universal basic income will not cure all social ills, and we must continue to offer prevention and intervention services for child abuse, mental health concerns, domestic violence, and addiction.

However, there are current models to support the idea that meeting someone's basic needs allows them to address more personal issues successfully. For example, Housing First is a growing movement to better serve individuals who simultaneously experience mental illness, substance abuse, and homelessness (sometimes referred to as co-occurring disorders or comorbidity). Traditionally, homeless shelters and transitional housing programs make sobriety a requirement to remain sheltered. This requirement conflicts with the truth that full recovery is a long road and often includes multiple relapses (SAMHSA, 2019). But if clients are kicked out of shelters when they relapse, the stress of living on the streets can make it even more difficult to maintain sobriety. Instead, Housing First programs accept the reality of relapse and remove rigid requirements for sobriety. In these programs, participants maintain more stable housing, report greater feelings of agency (Tsemberis, Gulcur, & Nakae, 2004), and in some studies, have lower rates of substance use than participants of sobriety-dependent housing programs (Padgett, Stanhope, Henwood, & Stefancic, 2011).

Basic Income and Behavior

A primary advantage of a UBI is that it does not attempt to influence human behavior, which we know is difficult, often poorly done, and a dangerous intrusion into the personal liberty of already marginalized people. UBI merely provides an income floor for every citizen. However, it is still essential for voters and policymakers to know that basic income pilot data do not indicate increases in undesirable social behavior. The basic income experiments of the 1960s and '70s lost a great deal of political support after early data reported increased divorce rates among recipients. Later evaluation of the data discovered that this finding was the result of an analysis error (Marinescu, 2017). In general, the North American experiments showed little effect on marriage or divorce rates (Marinescu, 2017). However, basic income pilots in developing countries have found that female recipients marry at a later age, have fewer children, and report "less unwanted sexual activity" (Standing, 2017).

Further, multiple studies have found a lack of support for the notion that the poor will spend unconditional assistance on things like alcohol, drugs, or cigarettes (Blattman & Niehaus, 2014; Evans & Popova, 2016). A pilot of 1000 people in Namibia discovered that crimes such as stealing food and illegal hunting decreased by 20% (Haarmann et al., 2008). In an Indian basic income pilot, spending on cigarettes and alcohol fell (Davala, Jhabvala, Standing, & Mehta, 2015). When researchers asked why this happened, Indian recipients explained that basic income gave the men better employment options (through small business and agriculture) and therefore less idle time for vices (Standing, 2017). This is a common theme among most basic income pilots: assistance is spent to improve the family's wellbeing and generally not on alcohol, tobacco, or drugs. Crime and domestic violence also decreased across many of the pilots (Standing, 2017).

In some studies, cash transfers were labeled as conditional, meaning that they were designated for a specific purpose such as school fees. A review of 165 conditional and unconditional cash transfer studies in multiple countries found that conditional transfers were sometimes associated with better outcomes (health and education), but stressing the importance of medical care, nutrition, and education to recipients may be just as effective as making it a condition of receipt (Hagen-Zanker et al., 2016).

The American welfare system is not alone in bungling its efforts to "intervene" in the lives of people living in poverty. The world of international aid is replete with examples of inept and paternalistic attempts to address global poverty. In 2005, for example, great excitement was generated for the Play Pump, which is a merry-go-round of sorts for African school children that pumps clean drinking water. The program failed when it was discovered that children needed to spin the pump nearly four hours straight to produce meaningful amounts of water and that the expensive pumps often broke down while villagers were never trained in how to maintain them (UNICEF, 2007). Social enterprises like Tom's Shoes, which donates a pair of shoes to children in developing countries for every pair sold, have been criticized for taking away jobs from local cobblers and other small businesses (Wharton School of Business, 2015).

It is much simpler and more effective to stop assuming that we know what impoverished communities need and let them make their own decisions. Personal and family decision making is complex and nearly impossible to engineer with large-scale policy interventions. The only thing stopping American public policy from accepting this reality is our dogged belief that low-income populations are incapable of making good decisions. We may no longer forcibly sterilize them or assign church representatives to follow their every move, but our continued inability to see human beings in poverty as actual human beings is no less harmful, ineffective and ultimately, a waste of resources.

References

Administration for Children and Families. (2018, November 20). *Characteristics and Financial Circumstances of TANF Recipients, Fiscal Year 2017*. Retrieved May 14, 2019, from Office of Family Assistance | ACF website: https://www.acf.hhs.gov/ofa/resource/characteristics-and-financial-circumstances-of-tanf-recipients-fiscal-year-2017

Aussenberg, R. A. (2018). *Errors and Fraud in the Supplemental Nutrition Assistance Program (SNAP)* (p. 64). Retrieved from Congressional Research Service Website: https://fas.org/sgp/crs/misc/R45147.pdf

Bitler, M. P., Gelbach, J. B., Hoynes, H. W., & Zavodny, M. (2004). The Impact of Welfare Reform on Marriage and Divorce. *Demography, 41*(2), 213–236.

Blattman, C., & Niehaus, P. (2014). Show Them the Money: Why Giving Cash Helps Alleviate Poverty. *Foreign Affairs, 93*(3), 117–126.

Bloom, D., Loprest, P. J., & Zedlewski, S. R. (2012). *TANF Recipients with Barriers to Employment*. Retrieved from Urban Institute Website: https://www.urban.org/research/publication/tanf-recipients-barriers-employment

Cancian, M., Meyer, D. R., & Caspar, E. (2008). Welfare and Child Support: Complements, Not Substitutes. *Journal of Policy Analysis and Management, 27*(2), 354–375.

Cancian, M., Meyer, D. R., & Wu, C.-F. (2005). After the Revolution: Welfare Patterns Since TANF Implementation. *Social Work Research, 29*(4), 199–214. https://doi.org/10.1093/swr/29.4.199.

Center for Substance Abuse Treatment. (2009). *Chapter 7: Substance Abuse Treatment for Women.* Retrieved from https://www.ncbi.nlm.nih.gov/books/NBK83257/

Cherlin, A. J., & Fomby, P. (2004). Welfare, Work, and Changes in Mothers' Living Arrangements in Low-Income Families. *Population Research and Policy Review, 23*(5/6), 543–565.

Cronquist, K., & Lauffer, S. (2019). *Characteristics of Supplemental Nutrition Assistance Program Households: Fiscal Year 2017* (No. SNAP-18-CHAR) (p. 153). Washington, DC: US Department of Agriculture.

Dallas News. (2013). *Editorial: No Drug Tests for Welfare; Texas Should Heed Florida's Lesson.* Retrieved January 30, 2018, from https://www.dallasnews.com/opinion/editorials/2013/03/26/editorial-no-drug-tests-for-welfare-texas-should-heed-floridas-lesson

Davala, S., Jhabvala, R., Standing, G., & Mehta, S. K. (2015). Basic Income: A Transformative Policy for India. London/New Delhi: Bloomsbury Academic.

Evans, D. K., & Popova, A. (2016). Cash Transfers and Temptation Goods. *Economic Development and Cultural Change, 65*(2), 189–221. https://doi.org/10.1086/689575.

Falk, G. (2016). *Temporary Assistance for Needy Families (TANF): Size and Characteristics of the Cash Assistance Caseload* (p. 21). Retrieved from Congressional Research Service Website: https://fas.org/sgp/crs/misc/R43187.pdf

Farber, S. A. (2008). U.S. Scientists' Role in the Eugenics Movement (1907–1939): A Contemporary Biologist's Perspective. *Zebrafish, 5*(4), 243–245. https://doi.org/10.1089/zeb.2008.0576.

Foster, A., & Rojas, A. (2018). Program Participation and Spending Patterns of Families Receiving Government Means-Tested Assistance. *Monthly Labor Review.* https://doi.org/10.21916/mlr.2018.3.

Fryar, G., Jordan, E., & Devooght, K. (2017). *Supporting Young People Transitioning from Foster Care: Findings from a National Survey.* Retrieved from Child Trends Website: https://www.childtrends.org/publications/supporting-young-people-transitioning-foster-care-findings-national-survey

Haarmann, C., Haarmann, D., Jauch, H., Shindonola-Mote, H., Nattrass, N., Samson, M., & Standing, G. (2008). *Towards a Basic Income Grant for All: Basic Income Grant Pilot Project Assessment Report, September 2008.* Retrieved from NANGOF Website: http://www.bignam.org/Publications/BIG_Assessment_report_08a.pdf

Hagen-Zanker, J., Bastagli, F., Harman, L., Barca, V., Sturge, G., & Schmidt, T. (2016). *Understanding the Impact of Cash Transfers: The Evidence* (p. 8). London: Overseas Development Institute.

Hamilton, L. (2016). Incentives in the Temporary Assistance for Needy Families Program: A Review of the Literature. *Poverty & Public Policy, 8*(2), 141–149. https://doi.org/10.1002/pop4.134.

Jackson, V. (2004). Residential Treatment for Parents and Their Children: The Village Experience. *Science & Practice Perspectives, 2*(2), 44–53.

Jacobs, K., Perry, I. E., & MacGillvary, J. (2015, April 13). *The High Public Cost of Low Wages*. Retrieved May 13, 2019, from Center for Labor Research and Education Website: http://laborcenter.berkeley.edu/the-high-public-cost-of-low-wages/

Kearney, M. S. (2004). Is There an Effect of Incremental Welfare Benefits on Fertility Behavior? A Look at the Family Cap. *The Journal of Human Resources, 39*(2), 295–325. https://doi.org/10.2307/3559016.

Larson, A. M., Singh, S., & Lewis, C. (2011). Sanctions and Education Outcomes for Children in TANF Families. *Child & Youth Services, 32*(3), 180–199.

Livingston, G. (2015). *Family Size Among Mothers | Pew Research Center*. Retrieved from Pew Research Center Website: https://www.pewsocialtrends.org/2015/05/07/family-size-among-mothers/

Lopoo, L. M., & DeLeire, T. (2006). Did Welfare Reform Influence the Fertility of Young Teens? *Journal of Policy Analysis and Management, 25*(2), 275–298.

Lyle, L. (2012). Florida's Legislation Mandating Suspicionless Drug Testing of TANF Beneficiaries: The Constitutionality and Efficacy of Implementing Drug Testing Requirements on the Welfare Population. *Tennessee Journal of Law & Policy, 8*, 68–85.

Mani, A., Mullainathan, S., Shafir, E., & Zhao, J. (2013). Poverty Impedes Cognitive Function. *Science, 341*(6149), 976–980. https://doi.org/10.1126/science.1238041.

Marinescu, I. (2017). *No Strings Attached: The Behavioral Effects of U.S. Unconditional Cash Transfer Programs*. Retrieved from Roosevelt Institute Website: http://rooseveltinstitute.org/wp-content/uploads/2017/05/No-Strings-Attached-050417-1.pdf

Minna Stern, A. (2016, January 7). *That Time the United States Sterilized 60,000 of Its Citizens*. Retrieved May 13, 2019, from HuffPost Website: https://www.huffpost.com/entry/sterilization-united-states_n_568f35f2e4b0c8beacf68713

Mullainathan, S., & Shafir, E. (2013). *Scarcity: Why Having Too Little Means so Much*. New York: Times Books.

Murray, C. (2008). *Losing Ground: American Social Policy, 1950–1980, 10th Anniversary Edition*. New York: Basic Books.

Oh, S., DiNitto, D. M., & Kim, Y. (2018). Substance Use and Use Disorders and Treatment Receipt Among Adults in Families Receiving Temporary Assistance for Needy Families (TANF), 2003–2014. *Addictive Behaviors, 85*, 173–179. https://doi.org/10.1016/j.addbeh.2018.06.014.

Padgett, D. K., Stanhope, V., Henwood, B. F., & Stefancic, A. (2011). Substance Use Outcomes Among Homeless Clients with Serious Mental Illness: Comparing Housing First with Treatment First Programs. *Community Mental Health Journal, 47*(2), 227–232. https://doi.org/10.1007/s10597-009-9283-7.

Pierson-Balik, D. A. (2003). Race, Class, and Gender in Punitive Welfare Reform: Social Eugenics and Welfare Policy. *Race, Gender & Class, 10*(1), 11–30. Retrieved from JSTOR.

Price, M. (2013, August 23). *Only 12 Test Positive in Utah Welfare Drug Screening*. Retrieved May 1, 2019, from https://www.ksl.com/article/26559995/only-12-test-positive-in-utah-welfare-drug-screening

Ridzi, F., & London, A. S. (2006). "It's Great When People Don't Even Have Their Welfare Cases Opened": TANF Diversion as Process and Lesson. *Review of Policy Research, 23*(3), 725–743. https://doi.org/10.1111/j.1541-1338.2006.00226.x.

Rockhill, A., Green, B., & Newton-Curtis, L. (2007). Accessing Substance Abuse Treatment: Issues for Parents Involved with Child Welfare Services. *Child Welfare, 87*(3), 63–93.

Rose, J. (n.d.). *A Brutal Chapter in North Carolina's Eugenics Past*. In *All Things Considered*. Retrieved from https://www.npr.org/2011/12/28/144375339/a-brutal-chapter-in-north-carolinas-eugenics-past

SAMHSA. (2019, January 14). *Recovery and Recovery Support [Text]*. Retrieved July 30, 2019, from Substance Abuse and Mental Health Services Administration Website: https://www.samhsa.gov/find-help/recovery

Seccombe, K., Walters, K. B., & James, D. (1999). "Welfare Mothers" Welcome Reform, Urge Compassion. *Family Relations, 48*(2), 197–206. https://doi.org/10.2307/585084.

Standing, G. (2017). *Basic Income: A Guide for the Open-Minded*. New Haven, CT/London: Yale University Press.

Swann, C. A., & Sylvester, M. S. (2006). The Foster Care Crisis: What Caused Caseloads to Grow? *Demography, 43*(2), 309–335.

Taylor, T., Gross, C. L., & Towne-Roese, J. K. (2016). Program Barriers and Challenges to Self-Sufficiency: A Qualitative Analysis of Ohio Welfare-to-Work Program Manager Identity. *Critical Sociology, 42*(7–8), 1125–1141. https://doi.org/10.1177/0896920515569084.

TEDx Talks. (2011). *Living Under Scarcity*. Retrieved from https://www.youtube.com/watch?v=gV1ESN8NGh8

Tirado, L. (2015). *Hand to Mouth: Living in Bootstrap America*. New York: Penguin.

Tsemberis, S., Gulcur, L., & Nakae, M. (2004). Housing First, Consumer Choice, and Harm Reduction for Homeless Individuals with a Dual Diagnosis. *American Journal of Public Health, 94*(4), 651–656. https://doi.org/10.2105/AJPH.94.4.651.

UNICEF. (2007). *An Evaluation of the PlayPump® Water System as an Appropriate Technology for Water, Sanitation and Hygiene Programmes*. Retrieved from UNICEF Website: https://www-tc.pbs.org/frontlineworld/stories/southernafrica904/flash/pdf/unicef_pp_report.pdf

Urban Institute. (2018). *The Welfare Rules Database*. Retrieved June 27, 2018, from https://wrd.urban.org/wrd/Query/query.cfm

US Department of Health and Human Services. (2012, March). *Overview of Immigrants' Eligibility for SNAP, TANF, Medicaid, and CHIP*. Retrieved May 24, 2019, from ASPE Website: https://aspe.hhs.gov/basic-report/overview-immigrants-eligibility-snap-tanf-medicaid-and-chip

US Government Accountability Office. (2019). *High Risk: Medicare Program & Improper Payments*. Retrieved from https://www.gao.gov/highrisk/medicare_program/why_did_study

Wallace, G. L. (2009). The Effects of Family Caps on the Subsequent Fertility Decisions of Never-Married Mothers. *Journal of Population Research, 26*(1), 73–101.

Wharton School of Business. (2015, February 16). *The One-for-One Business Model: Avoiding Unintended Consequences [University of Pennsylvania]*. Retrieved May 20, 2019, from https://knowledge.wharton.upenn.edu/article/one-one-business-model-social-impact-avoiding-unintended-consequences/

CHAPTER 4

Assets and Household Stability

Leah Hamilton, David Rothwell, Jin Huang, Yunju Nam, and Taylor Dollar

Abstract The ownership of assets is a more important component for escaping generational poverty than even income. Assets have the power to send children to college, purchase a home, start a small business, and provide insulation from minor emergencies that can devastate financially vulnerable families. However, most current welfare programs discourage savings by implementing low caps on assets for eligibility. While some fear that increasing asset limits would cause an overloaded welfare system and encourage dependence, the opposite appears to be true. Further, low-income families are more likely to have savings and own a vehicle in states with relatively liberal limits. The reasons for this are intuitive. Allowing families to build their own safety nets makes them less likely to need outside assistance.

Keywords Assets • Wealth • Basic income • Welfare • Temporary Assistance to Needy Families

---

An earlier version of this chapter appeared as Hamilton, L., Rothwell, D., Huang, J., Nam, Y., & Dollar, T. (2019). Guarding public coffers or trapping the poor? The role of public assistance asset limits in program efficacy and family economic well-being. *Poverty & Public Policy, 11*(1–2), 12–30. https://doi.org/10.1002/pop4.244.

L. Hamilton, *Welfare Doesn't Work*, Exploring the Basic Income Guarantee, https://doi.org/10.1007/978-3-030-37121-0_4

Wealth Inequality in America

While income inequality in America is a significant concern, the growing wealth divide is the real story. Income helps people pay the bills, but savings and household assets are how families send children to college, buy homes in "good" school districts, and ultimately ensure that future generations of their family have the privileges and opportunities that low-wealth families do not (Prosperity Now, 2013). A recent report by Georgetown University's Center on Education and Workforce found that the socioeconomic status of parents is a more important determinant of a child's life chances than even the child's intelligence. The authors state that "a child from the bottom quartile of socioeconomic status who has high test scores in kindergarten has only a three in ten chance of having a college education and a good entry-level job as a young adult, compared to a seven in ten chance for a child in the top quartile of socioeconomic status who has *low test scores* [emphasis added]" (Carnevale, Fasules, Quinn, & Campbell, 2019, p. 1).

Further, wealth has a generationally compounding effect. If one's parents bequeath them a home, the equity can be used for greater real estate or other self-optimizing investments. For this reason, the consequences of hundreds of years of racial discrimination and exploitation are not simply wiped out by removing barriers to education and employment for modern day minorities. Because racial minorities, especially African Americans, were barred from jobs, educational opportunities, and homeownership for much of the twentieth century, these families were not able to build the intergenerational and compounding wealth that white families were. One study tracked 1700 American households from 1984 to 2009 and found that for every dollar increase in income in both white and black households, white families increased their household wealth by $5.19 compared to just 0.69 cents for black families (Shapiro, Meschede, & Osoro, 2013). The result of this lag in wealth building is striking. White and black average household wealth in 2016 was $171,000 and $17,100, respectively. Even middle-income African American households carry just one-quarter of the average wealth of middle-income white households (Kochhar & Fry, 2014).

Do the Poor Lack Financial Literacy?

A common myth seen in the media, in policy debates, and in my classroom is the idea that people in poverty lack basic financial management skills, and providing universal financial literacy training would significantly improve poverty. A meta-analysis of 168 empirical studies found that receiving financial literacy training only predicted 0.1% of the difference in people's financial decision making. The effect was even smaller for low-income people (Fernandes, Lynch, & Netemeyer, 2014). Much stronger predictors of financial literacy and decision making are education and income (Murphy, 2013). Not surprisingly, it is easier to have savings and make sound financial decisions when you earn a living wage. Further, no amount of financial literacy training can help you learn how to stretch an income that has not kept pace with the cost of living in decades (Williams & Rosenstock, 2015).

While it is true that those with higher incomes save at an increased rate (Dynan, Skinner, & Zeldes, 2004), this does not mean that low-income households are unaware of the benefits or lack the skills to save. In addition to having less disposable income to save, many low-income households continue to carry a distrust of financial institutions for very good, historical reasons. The poor are less likely to have bank accounts, partially because they know that, even today, they are more likely to be victims of predatory lending (Stiglitz, 2012) and unfair bank fees (Mullainathan & Shafir, 2010). But when given access to safe vehicles for savings, the poor can and do save (Schreiner & Sherraden, 2006).

The Policy Landscape

While eligibility criteria for means-tested safety net programs in the United States, such as TANF, SNAP, Medicaid, and Supplemental Security Income (SSI) exist to ensure that scarce public resources go to those most in need, limits on participant assets arguably create additional barriers to long-term economic security and household financial development that exacerbate wealth inequality. It is important to note that the policy of setting asset limits for low-income populations stands in contrast to policies that exist to encourage asset accumulation among the middle and upper classes such as tax-sheltered retirement accounts, mortgage interest deductions, and relatively low capital gains taxes.

Temporary Assistance for Needy Families

As discussed in previous chapters, the history of America's means-tested cash assistance program has closely followed the progression of national politics, expanding in the 1950s and 1960s, contracting severely in the 1980s, and then devolving to state control during the mid-1990s Conservative Revolution. Federally mandated asset limits for eligibility ($1500 per household member) were introduced to the Aid to Families with Dependent Children (AFDC) program in 1955, although states were allowed to set lower limits (Powers, 1998). These limits increased to $2000 per household member in 1960, with a household maximum of $8000. In 1981, Reagan's Omnibus Reconciliation Act decreased limits to $1000 per household (Hamilton, Alexander-Eitzman, & Royal, 2014). When TANF replaced AFDC in 1996, federal limits were removed, allowing states to create their own income and asset eligibility criteria (Powers, 1998). As a result, state-by-state variation in welfare policy is currently wider than across many European countries (Bruch, Meyers, & Gornick, 2018).

Most states have either maintained their 1980s asset limits or made moderate increases. However, a small number of states have eliminated the limit altogether. The first state to remove resource testing for TANF was Ohio in 1997 (Rand, 2007), followed by Virginia in 2004, Alabama and Louisiana in 2008, Maryland in 2010, Colorado in 2011, Hawaii in 2013, and Illinois in 2014 (Prosperity Now, 2018). The remaining limits range from $1000 to $10,000, with the majority of states setting the threshold at or below $2500 (Pew Charitable Trusts, 2016). Most states exclude "illiquid" assets, such as a home but other categories of assets such as Individual Development Accounts, vehicles, retirement accounts, and Child Development Accounts are treated differently by each state.

Supplemental Nutrition Assistance Program/Food Stamps

The Department of Agriculture federally administers the SNAP program, which plays a critical component of the social safety net, especially during times of economic recession. For example, between 2000 and 2014, the reach of SNAP tripled from 5% to 15% of the population (Wiseman, 2017). For families to become eligible for SNAP, gross household income must fall below 130% of the federal poverty line. Additionally, household asset limits are $2250 with higher amounts if at least one person is age 60 or older, or disabled (United States Department of Agriculture, 2017a). If participants also receive SSI or TANF, their asset limits for SNAP are waived in 34 states (Prosperity Now, 2018; Ratcliffe, McKernan, Wheaton, & Kalish, 2016). Most retirement plans such as 401(k), 403(b), myRA, and Thrift Savings Plans are exempt from the asset tests of SNAP (United States Department of Agriculture, 2017b). States have discretion in determining motor vehicles as assets. As of 2017, over 60% of states exclude all vehicle values entirely (United States Department of Agriculture, 2017a).

Medicaid

Administered jointly by states and the federal government, Medicaid is the largest health insurer in the United States, covering more than 75 million Americans as of 2017 (Centers for Medicare & Medicaid Services, n.d.). The next largest insurer, United Health, covers less than 50 million (Haefner, 2019). The 2013 Affordable Care Act (ACA) set income eligibility standard at 133% of the federal poverty line and eliminated asset tests (Center for Medicaid and Medicaid Services, 2014). Before the ACA, Medicaid income and resource limits were set by states within specific federal parameters; however, many states had already removed asset limits for applicant children before 2013 (Medicaid Program; Eligibility Changes Under the Affordable Care Act of 2010, 2012), and a few states eliminated limits for parents as well (Cohen Ross, Jarlenski, Artiga, & Marks, 2009). A 2012 study reported an average state asset limit of $4000 (Sommers, Tomasi, Swartz, & Epstein, 2012). Resource limits for Medicaid nursing home and home and community-based care were unchanged by the ACA and remain around $2000 in most states (Kassner & Shirey, 2000; Musumeci, 2014).

Supplemental Security Income

The Supplemental Security Income (SSI) program is a means-tested program that supplies cash assistance to individuals who fall below certain income and asset tests, are blind, or disabled. SSI should not be confused with Social Security Disability Insurance (SSDI), which is designed for recipients with sufficient work credits through the Federal Insurance Contributions Act (better known as FICA) payroll deduction program and does not use asset tests in eligibility determination (Social Security

Administration, 2017). The federal asset limit for SSI was set at $2000 per individual and $3000 per couple in 1989 and has not changed since that time (Social Security Administration, 2016). The SSA defines resources as cash, savings, stocks and bonds, land, vehicles, life insurance, personal property, or any other asset that can be sold or turned into food and shelter (Social Security Administration, 2019). The land or property that an individual or family lives on is exempt as are burial spaces or funds, household goods and personal effects such as wedding rings, and one vehicle as long as it functions for transportation. A few other resources do not count, with certain stipulations. For example, retroactive SSI, Social Security benefits, and grants or scholarships are exempt from resource testing for nine months after receipt.

In 2014, Congress passed the ABLE Act, which created special savings accounts for individuals with disabilities. These accounts are tax-sheltered and are only applicable to "disability-related expenses" (Autism Speaks, 2014). Contributions to these accounts do not count toward asset limits for SSI eligibility. However, the restrictions on these accounts mean that many with disabilities still lack the opportunity to build assets. As one MTurker with a disability explained, "Being limited to a maximum of $2000 in assets ensures that I can never save money."

Implications of Asset Limits

Restrictive asset tests emerged as a policy issue in the 1990s as the role of assets in long-term economic development became more clearly recognized by researchers (Nam, McKernan, & Ratcliffe, 2008; Sherraden, 1991). Asset limits have both theoretical and real-world consequences for program participation, asset holdings, financial behaviors, employment, and vehicle ownership among low-income households. These tests also have significant implications for the administrative costs associated with poverty alleviation programs.

Program Participation

Restrictive asset tests may influence low-income families' safety net program participation in two opposing directions. In the short term, strict limits may reduce participation by imposing obstacles, especially for those with modest assets (Nam et al., 2008). In the long term, low asset thresholds may *increase* low-income families' long-term program participation by discouraging them from acquiring the economic means for stable employment (e.g., a reliable automobile) or from saving for emergencies (Rice & Bansak, 2014), which traps low-income families in poverty and long-term reliance on public assistance.

When looking at short-term impacts, restrictive asset tests negatively impact families' safety net program participation in multiple ways. First, restrictive asset tests reduce participation by disqualifying income-eligible families with modest assets (Nam et al., 2008). Second, strict asset tests increase the time and efforts needed to apply for assistance. Required time, effort, and the risk of being rejected can discourage income-eligible families from even applying, especially those whose asset levels are close to asset thresholds. Furthermore, asset tests may even deter eligible families without assets from applying for programs because the asset-eligibility verifying process is burdensome and intrusive: asset tests require applicants to prepare a series of private documents, including bank statements and vehicle information (Nam et al., 2008; O'Brien, 2008; Pavetti, Maloy, & Schott, 2002). Third, stringent asset tests often confuse low-income families about their eligibility. A substantial proportion of eligible families decide not to apply for safety net programs because they falsely believe that they are ineligible (Bartlett, Burstein, & Hamilton, 2004).

Contrary to short-term impacts, strict asset tests likely *increase* low-income families' safety net program participation in the long term. Restrictive asset tests prohibit program beneficiaries from owning assets beyond certain levels. As a result, recipients are discouraged from acquiring the economic means for stable employment and long-term development (e.g., automobiles or small businesses) or to save for emergencies. The lack of asset ownership may provide an incentive for families to stay on safety net programs for longer periods of time. Even among those who exit safety net programs, low levels of emergency savings often drive them to return to these programs for minor economic shocks, such as short-term layoffs or vehicle problems (a "churning" phenomenon that refers to returning to safety net programs after a very short-term exit) (McKernan, Ratcliffe, & Nam, 2010; Rice & Bansak, 2014). Relaxing asset limits reduces SNAP churn by 26% and does not affect the length of time people stay on SNAP (Mabli & Ohls, 2015; Ratcliffe et al., 2016).

Asset Holdings and Financial Behaviors

The true impacts of asset rules on savings and asset accumulation among low-income families is not entirely clear. While some research indicates that low asset limits are associated with lower rates savings among low-income families, other research has found no association (Hamilton, 2017). There are multiple potential explanations for these conflicting findings. Some authors (Hurst & Ziliak, 2006) argue that a substantial proportion of low-income households already have very few assets; therefore, low asset tests have little impact in practice. Further, the period under examination seems to affect the outcome. Research conducted in periods of economic expansion suggests that liberalizing asset limits has a positive effect on the savings rates of low-income families (Nam, 2008), but studies conducted during the Great Recession found little impact (Hamilton, 2017). Significant swings in the economy are probably equally relevant to the savings behavior of low-income families as welfare eligibility rules.

Finally, the removal of such an institutional barrier in one program does not necessarily and automatically result in increased savings and assets. There may be other policy barriers against low-income households' saving efforts and asset building. For example, even with related asset tests under AFDC/TANF, low-income families may still be constrained by the asset limits of other means-tested programs (such as SNAP or SSI). The effect of relaxed TANF asset rules on savings then could be restricted by these other barriers. Without a comprehensive institutional system supporting asset building among disadvantaged populations, the change of asset tests in one single program may not be sufficient to promote savings.

Labor Market Outcomes

The desire to save often motivates individuals to improve their labor market outcomes because earnings are usually the primary means of savings among low and moderate-income populations. As a result, restrictive asset tests could theoretically discourage low-income individuals from pursuing work that pays a relatively higher wage. Also, asset tests may have indirect impacts. According to the "asset-effect hypothesis," assets have positive economic, psychological, and social impacts: assets often play critical roles in individuals' human capital attainment via financing education and training; assets promote future orientation by assisting individuals to see viable and hopeful futures; and assets offer buffers against short-term economic pressures and allow individuals not to make costly financial decisions (e.g., declining a suboptimal immediate job offer when an optimal job offer is anticipated later) (Nam, Huang, & Sherraden, 2004; Paxton, 2001; Sherraden, 1991). Considering that all these factors (human capital attainment, future orientation, and prudent risk-taking) are closely related to labor market outcomes, asset tests may influence low-income individuals' labor market outcomes negatively. Although there is not a substantial body of support for the direct relationship between assets limits and employment, several studies provide indirect evidence that relaxed asset rules, specifically relating to vehicle assets, may promote employment through their impacts on vehicle ownership.

Vehicle Ownership

Owning a reliable vehicle is strongly linked to increased labor market participation, work hours, and earnings among low-income individuals. Vehicle ownership often decreases commute time and frees up time for other activities such as caring for children, which is critical for labor market participation decisions among substantial portions of low-income individuals, including single mothers receiving cash assistance (Bansak, Mattson, & Rice, 2010). Furthermore, vehicle ownership may improve otherwise grim job prospects among inner-city or rural low-income individuals who live far from decent jobs or reliable public transportation (Massey & Denton, 1993; Raphael & Stoll, 2001; Wilson, 1997). A transportation problem (lack of a vehicle or driver's license) is one of the most common barriers to employment among safety net beneficiaries (Danziger et al., 2000). Accordingly, restrictive asset tests likely deter low-income individuals' vehicle ownership, which may have negative impacts on their labor market outcomes. One MTurker and former recipient of multiple welfare programs explained, "It was hard to get ahead, we desperately needed a car but could never get far enough ahead to buy one." While findings are mixed on the relationship between asset limits and savings, the effects to vehicle ownership is straightforward. Several studies have discovered that relaxing vehicle limits in TANF and SNAP leads to increases in vehicle ownership and vehicle value among low-income families (Baek & Raschke, 2016; McKernan et al., 2010; Owens & Baum, 2012; Rice & Bansak, 2014; Sullivan, 2006).

Administrative Costs

Asset tests affect government spending through two different mechanisms: (1) caseloads and (2) administrative costs. The impacts to caseloads are complex. In the short-term, asset tests likely reduce caseloads for safety net programs because they disqualify income-eligible families with modest assets, driving down total caseload numbers. However, restrictive asset tests may increase long-term caseloads if they discourage low-income families' saving and asset accumulation and deter their long-term economic development (Bansak et al., 2010; Nam, 2008).

A small number of studies have empirically investigated the impacts of constricting or expanding asset limits on public assistance program caseloads. Using data from five states that increased asset limits to $10,000 or eliminated nonvehicle asset limits during the Great Recession, one study found that relaxed asset tests did not increase caseloads or the rate of caseload growth (Hamilton et al., 2014). Another found that increasing asset limits significantly increased states' TANF caseloads, but the impacts are small: the estimated mean increase was between 31 and 165 cases per 100,000 residents (Pew Charitable Trusts, 2016). The same study finds no significant increases in caseloads when asset limits are eliminated entirely. The interaction effects of asset limits and vehicle exemption in the latter study is noteworthy: when states exempt vehicles from asset tests, caseloads decline moderately. In other words, people move off of assistance when they are allowed to own reliable transportation. Analyses of SNAP also produce similar results to those on TANF: the average number of SNAP cases in states without an asset limit is only 407 more per 100,000 residents than that of states with an asset limit (Pew Charitable Trusts, 2016).

While asset tests may have very small or no effects on caseloads, they represent high administrative costs for safety net programs. Asset tests require caseworkers to review asset-related documents (e.g., bank statements) and estimate asset-values (e.g., vehicle values) to determine eligibility, which is complicated and time-consuming (McKernan et al., 2010; Sprague & Black, 2012). Administrative expenditures for TANF is 2% lower among states exempting at least one vehicle from asset limits (Pew Charitable Trusts, 2016).

In addition, strict asset tests may increase administrative costs through their impacts on program churn: cases that return to safety net programs after a short-term exit. Asset tests may disqualify beneficiaries for temporary increases in assets (e.g., a tax-return amount deposited into a bank account). These beneficiaries tend to use up their savings and assets quickly after they lose eligibility, which causes them to return to assistance programs. The costs associated with reopening cases caused by churn is about $80 per case, which is twice or three times that needed for recertification of ongoing cases (Mills et al., 2014; Pew Charitable Trusts, 2016).

Basic Income and Assets

Few of the basic income pilots to date have tracked participant financial assets. However, those that do provide promising results. In 2011, the nonprofit Give Directly launched a basic income experiment in poor, rural villages of Kenya. Over the course of 9 months, more than 500 low-income households received an average total of $709 USD in unconditional cash transfers. The study also followed hundreds of similar households for comparison. Four months after the pilot ended, household assets among recipients had increased significantly in comparison to the control group. Shockingly, the positive effects remained when researchers followed up three years later; families who received basic income even for this brief period had 40% more assets than comparison households. Significant assets included livestock, household appliances, motorbikes, and bicycles as these things can substantially improve quality of life and income prospects for rural Kenyans (Haushofer & Shapiro, 2018).

Surveys of recipients of the Alaska Permanent Fund and in the recent Ontario pilot discovered similar improvements to participant's financial health. When asked how they spend their dividend, 57% of Alaskans said that they either save it or use it to pay off debt (Isenberg, 2017). Half of the Ontario participants reported that the pilot had allowed them to begin saving, 46% were able to pay off debt, and nearly 65% felt less stress about unexpected expenses (Basic Income Canada Network, 2019).

- "I was able to get out from under payday loans. I was able to feel dignity in living and hope for being able to maybe buy a cheap car, pay off debt and not being looked down on by my neighbors."
- "I was able to pay arrear taxes owed to city otherwise possible foreclosure which was putting me in deep depression and was feeling suicidal."

- "I did not pay off all debt but am making headway."
- "It helped me pay my bills on time."
- "I saved money because of no late fees and not using credit."

In essence, modern government programs create two tiers of financial incentives: those discouraging savings among the poor (TANF, SNAP, and SSI) and those that encourage wealth building among middle- and upper-income citizens (401ks, mortgage deductions, and low capital gains taxes). Wealth inequality in America cannot be remediated if we do not remove this unfair and counterproductive system. With an unconditional basic income, we would finally allow low-income Americans the freedom to build wealth and improve the financial prospects of their children currently afforded only to those who already have enough income and assets to own a home, access employer provided retirement programs, or invest in stocks.

References

Autism Speaks. (2014, December 17). *10 Things to Know About the ABLE Act.* Retrieved January 22, 2018, from Autism Speaks Website: https://www.autismspeaks.org/news/news-item/10-things-know-about-able-act

Baek, D., & Raschke, C. (2016). The Impact of SNAP Vehicle Asset Limits on Household Asset Allocation. *Southern Economic Journal, 83*(1), 146–175. https://doi.org/10.1002/soej.12135.

Bansak, C., Mattson, H., & Rice, L. (2010). Cars, Employment, and Single Mothers: The Effect of Welfare Asset Restrictions. *Industrial Relations: A Journal of Economy and Society, 49*(3), 321–345. https://doi.org/10.1111/j.1468-232X.2010.00603.x.

Bartlett, S., Burstein, N., & Hamilton, W. (2004). *Food Stamp Program Access Study: Final Report* (No. E-FAN-03-013-3) (p. 482). Washington, DC: Food Assistance & Nutrition Research Program.

Basic Income Canada Network. (2019). *Signposts to Success: Report of a BICN Survey of Ontario Basic Income Recipients.* Retrieved from Basic Income Canada Network Website: https://www.basicincomecanada.org/time_for_national_action_new_report_shows_ontario_basic_income_pilot_was_on_track_to_success?fbclid=IwAR1BcwCr6pQ-kLHv_YRXddbK48jv2OLH9pGX-X1rU_946RB-Kvro2wvVrCg

Bruch, S. K., Meyers, M. K., & Gornick, J. C. (2018). The Consequences of Decentralization: Inequality in Safety Net Provision in the Post–Welfare Reform Era. *Social Service Review, 92*(1), 3–35. https://doi.org/10.1086/696132.

Carnevale, A. P., Fasules, M. L., Quinn, M. C., & Campbell, K. P. (2019). *Born to Win, Schooled to Lose: Why Equally Talented Students Don't Get Equal Chances to Be All They Can Be*. Retrieved from Center on Education and the Workforce Website: https://1gyhoq479ufd3yna29x7ubjn-wpengine.netdna-ssl.com/wp-content/uploads/ES-Born_to_win-schooled_to_lose.pdf

Center for Medicaid and Medicaid Services. (2014, February 21). *Application of Liens, Adjustments and Recoveries, Transfer-of-Asset Rules and Post Eligibility Income Rules to MAGI Individuals*. Retrieved from https://www.medicaid.gov/Federal-Policy-Guidance/Downloads/SMD-14-001.pdf

Centers for Medicare & Medicaid Services. (n.d.). *September 2017 Medicaid and CHIP Enrollment Data Highlights*. Retrieved December 13, 2017, from https://www.medicaid.gov/medicaid/program-information/medicaid-and-chip-enrollment-data/report-highlights/index.html

Cohen Ross, D., Jarlenski, M., Artiga, S., & Marks, C. (2009). *A Foundation for Health Reform: Findings of An Annual 50-State Survey of Eligibility Rules, Enrollment and Renewal Procedures and Cost-Sharing Practices in Medicaid and CHIP for Children and Parents During 2009*. Retrieved from Kaiser Family Foundation Website: https://www.kff.org/medicaid/report/a-foundation-for-health-reform-findings-of/

Danziger, S., Corcoran, M., Danzinger, S. K., Heflin, C., Kalil, A., Levin, J., & Tolman, R. (2000). Barriers to the Employment of Welfare Recipients. In R. Cherry & W. M. Rodgers III (Eds.), *Prosperity for All?: The Economic Boom and African Americans*. New York: Russell Sage Foundation.

Dynan, K. E., Skinner, J. S., & Zeldes, S. P. (2004). Do the Rich Save More? *Journal of Political Economy, 112*, 397–444.

Fernandes, D., Lynch, J. G., & Netemeyer, R. G. (2014). Financial Literacy, Financial Education, and Downstream Financial Behaviors. *Management Science, 60*(8), 1861–1883. https://doi.org/10.1287/mnsc.2013.1849.

Haefner, M. (2019, January 10). *America's Largest Health Insurers in 2018*. Retrieved August 17, 2019, from Beckers Hospital Review Website: https://www.beckershospitalreview.com/payer-issues/america-s-largest-health-insurers-in-2018.html

Hamilton, L. (2017). *Asset Limits in Public Assistance and Savings Behavior Among Low-Income Families*. Retrieved from Pew Charitable Trusts website: http://www.pewtrusts.org/~/media/assets/2017/09/asset_limits_in_public_assistance_and_savings_behavior_among_low_income_families.pdf

Hamilton, L., Alexander-Eitzman, B., & Royal, W. (2014). *Shelter from the Storm: TANF, Assets and the Great Recession*. Manuscript Submitted for Publication.

Haushofer, J., & Shapiro, J. (2018). *The Long-Term Impact of Unconditional Cash Transfers: Experimental Evidence from Kenya*. Retrieved from Busara Center for Behavioral Economics Website: https://jeremypshapiro.appspot.com/papers/Haushofer_Shapiro_UCT2_2018-01-30_paper_only.pdf

Hurst, E., & Ziliak, J. P. (2006). Do Welfare Asset Limits Affect Household Saving? *The Journal of Human Resources, 41*(1), 46–71.

Isenberg, T. J. (2017, June 28). *What a New Survey from Alaska Can Teach Us About Public Support for Basic Income.* Retrieved August 1, 2019, from Medium Website: https://medium.com/economicsecproj/what-a-new-survey-from-alaska-can-teach-us-about-public-support-for-basic-income-ccd0c3c16b42

Kassner, E., & Shirey, L. (2000). *Medicaid Financial Eligibility for Older People: State Variations in Access to Home and Community-Based Waiver and Nursing Home Services* (p. 32). Retrieved from AARP Website: https://assets.aarp.org/rgcenter/health/2000_06_medicaid.pdf

Kochhar, R., & Fry, R. (2014, December 12). *Wealth Inequality Has Widened Along Racial, Ethnic Lines Since End of Great Recession.* Retrieved January 3, 2017, from Pew Research Center Website: http://www.pewresearch.org/fact-tank/2014/12/12/racial-wealth-gaps-great-recession/

Mabli, J., & Ohls, J. (2015). Supplemental Nutrition Assistance Program Participation Is Associated with an Increase in Household Food Security in a National Evaluation. *The Journal of Nutrition, 145*(2), 344–351. https://doi.org/10.3945/jn.114.198697.

Massey, D. S., & Denton, N. A. (1993). *American Apartheid: Segregation and the Making of the Underclass* (1st Paperback ed.). Cambridge, MA: Harvard University Press.

McKernan, S.-M., Ratcliffe, C., & Nam, Y. (2010). The Effects of Welfare and Individual Development Account (IDA) Program Rules on Asset Holdings. *Social Science Research, 39*(1), 92–110. https://doi.org/10.1016/j.ssresearch.2009.07.008.

Medicaid Program; Eligibility Changes Under the Affordable Care Act of 2010. 42 CFR § §435.603(G) (2012).

Mills, G. B., Vericker, T., Koball, H., Lippold, K., Wheaton, L., & Elkin, S. (2014). *Understanding the Rates, Causes, and Costs of Churning in the Supplemental Nutrition Assistance Program (SNAP)* (p. 184). Retrieved from Urban Institute Website: https://www.urban.org/sites/default/files/publication/33566/413257-Understanding-the-Rates-Causes-and-Costs-of-Churning-in-the-Supplemental-Nutrition-Assistance-Program-SNAP-.PDF

Mullainathan, S., & Shafir, E. (2010). *Savings Policy and Decisionmaking in Low-Income Households* (No. 24; p. 4). Retrieved from National Poverty Center Website: https://pdfs.semanticscholar.org/47c1/8df72a1da9c7f547ad39228 3dcff3c476e9f.pdf

Murphy, J. L. (2013). Psychosocial Factors and Financial Literacy. *Social Security Bulletin, 73,* 73–82.

Musumeci, M. (2014). *The Affordable Care Act's Impact on Medicaid Eligibility, Enrollment, and Benefits for People with Disabilities.* Retrieved from Kaiser Family Foundation Website: https://www.kff.org/health-reform/issue-brief/

the-affordable-care-acts-impact-on-medicaid-eligibility-enrollment-and-benefits-for-people-with-disabilities/

Nam, Y. (2008). Welfare Reform and Asset Accumulation: Asset Limit Changes, Financial Assets, and Vehicle Ownership. *Social Science Quarterly, 89*(1), 133–154.

Nam, Y., Huang, J., & Sherraden, M. (2004). Asset Definitions. In S.-M. McKernan & M. Sherraden (Eds.), *Asset Building and Low-Income Families*. Washington, DC: Urban Institute Press.

Nam, Y., McKernan, S.-M., & Ratcliffe, C. (2008). Effects of Asset Tests and IDA Programs. In S.-M. McKernan & M. Sherraden (Eds.), *Asset Building and Low-Income Families*. Washington, DC: Urban Institute Press.

O'Brien, R. (2008). Ineligible to Save? Asset Limits and the Saving Behavior of Welfare Recipients. *Journal of Community Practice, 16*(2), 183–199. https://doi.org/10.1080/10705420801998003.

Owens, M. F., & Baum, C. L. (2012). The Effects of Welfare Vehicle Asset Rules on Vehicle Assets. *Applied Economics, 44*(13), 1603–1619. https://doi.org/10.1080/00036846.2010.548783.

Pavetti, L., Maloy, K., & Schott, L. (2002). *Promoting Medicaid and Food Stamp Participation: Establishing Eligibility Procedures That Support Participation and Meet Families' Needs* (p. 140). Retrieved from Mathematica Policy Research, Inc. Website: https://www.acf.hhs.gov/sites/default/files/opre/medicaid_fstamp.pdf

Paxton, W. (2001). The Asset-Effect: An Overview. In J. Bryner & W. Paxton (Eds.), *The Asset-Effect*. London: Institute for Public Policy Research.

Pew Charitable Trusts. (2016). *Do Limits on Family Assets Affect Participation in, Costs of TANF?* Retrieved from Pew Charitable Trusts Website: http://pew.org/29n0ICJ

Powers, E. T. (1998). Does Means-Testing Welfare Discourage Saving? Evidence from a Change in AFDC Policy in the United States. *Journal of Public Economics, 68*(1), 33–53.

Prosperity Now. (2013). *Why Assets Matter: An Overview of Research on Assets and Their Effect on Financial Stability and Economic Opportunity*. Retrieved from https://prosperitynow.org/files/PDFs/financial_capability_planning_guide/WhyAssetsMatter_2013updates.pdf

Prosperity Now. (2018). *Asset Limits in Public Benefit Programs*. Retrieved from https://scorecard.prosperitynow.org/data-by-issue

Rand, D. (2007). Reforming State Rules on Asset Limits: How to Remove Barriers to Saving and Asset Accumulation in Public Benefit Programs. *Clearinghouse REVIEW Journal of Poverty Law and Policy*, (March–April), 625–636.

Raphael, S., & Stoll, M. A. (2001). Can Boosting Minority Car-Ownership Rates Narrow Inter-Racial Employment Gaps? *Brookings-Wharton Papers on Urban Affairs, 2001*(1), 99–145. https://doi.org/10.1353/urb.2001.0013.

Ratcliffe, C., McKernan, S.-M., Wheaton, L., & Kalish, E. C. (2016, July 26). *The Unintended Consequences of SNAP Asset Limits*. Retrieved December 24, 2016, from Urban Institute Website: http://www.urban.org/research/publication/unintended-consequences-snap-asset-limits

Rice, L., & Bansak, C. (2014). The Effect of Welfare Asset Rules on Auto Ownership, Employment, and Welfare Participation: A Longitudinal Analysis. *Contemporary Economic Policy, 32*(2), 306–333.

Schreiner, M., & Sherraden, M. (2006). *Can the Poor Save?: Saving and Asset Building in Individual Development Accounts*. New Brunswick, NJ: Transaction Publishers.

Shapiro, T., Meschede, T., & Osoro, S. (2013). *The Roots of the Widening Racial Wealth Gap: Explaining the Black-White Economic Divide*. Retrieved from Institute on Assets and Social Policy Website: http://health-equity.lib.umd.edu/4120/1/racialwealthgapbrief.pdf

Sherraden, M. (1991). *Assets and the Poor: A New American Welfare Policy*. New York: M E Sharpe Inc.

Social Security Administration. (2016). *Annual Statistical Supplement*. Retrieved from https://www.ssa.gov/policy/docs/statcomps/supplement/2016/ssi.pdf

Social Security Administration. (2017). *Comparison of the SSDI and SSI Disability Programs*. Retrieved November 28, 2017, from https://www.ssa.gov/redbook/eng/overview-disability.htm

Social Security Administration. (2019). *Understanding Supplemental Security Income Resources*. Retrieved from https://www.ssa.gov/ssi/text-resources-ussi.htm

Sommers, B. D., Tomasi, M. R., Swartz, K., & Epstein, A. M. (2012). Reasons for the Wide Variation in Medicaid Participation Rates Among States Hold Lessons for Coverage Expansion in 2014. *Health Affairs, 31*(5), 909–919. https://doi.org/10.1377/hlthaff.2011.0977.

Sprague, A., & Black, A. (2012). *State Asset Limit Reforms and Implications for Federal Policy*. Retrieved from http://assets.newamerica.net/sites/newamerica.net/files/policydocs/SpragueBlackFinal10.31.12.pdf

Stiglitz, J. E. (2012). *The Price of Inequality: How Today's Divided Society Endangers Our Future* (1st ed.). New York: W. W. Norton & Company.

Sullivan, J. (2006). Welfare Reform, Saving, and Vehicle Ownership: Do Asset Limits and Vehicle Exemptions Matter? *Journal of Human Resources, 41*(1), 73–105.

United States Department of Agriculture. (2017a). *Am I Eligible for SNAP? | Food and Nutrition Service*. Retrieved April 19, 2018, from https://www.fns.usda.gov/snap/eligibility

United States Department of Agriculture. (2017b). *Updated Retirement Account Exclusions from Resources*. Retrieved from https://fns-prod.azureedge.net/sites/default/files/snap/Memo-Updated-Retirement-Account-Exclusions-From-Resources.pdf

Williams, J. A. R., & Rosenstock, L. (2015). Squeezing Blood from a Stone: How Income Inequality Affects the Health of the American Workforce. *American Journal of Public Health, 105*(4), 616–621. https://doi.org/10.2105/AJPH.2014.302424.

Wilson, W. J. (1997). *When Work Disappears: The World of the New Urban Poor* (1st ed.). New York: Vintage.

Wiseman, M. (2017). *The Supplemental Nutrition Assistance Program* (IRP Discussion Paper No. 1435–17). Retrieved from University of Wisconsin-Madison Website: https://www.irp.wisc.edu/publications/dps/pdfs/dp143517.pdf

CHAPTER 5

The Lives of Low-Income Women

Abstract American welfare policies have historically placed sexist and often racist expectations on the lives and reproduction of low-income women, who are frequently stigmatized when seeking assistance. Further, our crumbling social safety net has contributed to the feminization of poverty in America. Universal basic income has the potential to create a more egalitarian footing for women in society and allow families to make the work, marriage, childcare, and reproductive decisions that are right for them. It would also better support the millions of hours of unpaid care work that women contribute to the economy each year.

Keywords Women • Welfare • Basic income • Reproduction • Temporary Assistance to Needy Families

Up to this point, we have described the purposes of the welfare state as maintaining social order and providing cheap labor for industry (especially black labor). But it has also served another purpose: controlling the marital, sexual, and reproductive decisions of poor and minority women. The principle of "less eligibility," in which welfare is designed to pay less than the lowest paying job is twofold for women. It is designed to incentivize both work *and* marriage to a male breadwinner (Abramovitz, 1996). The very existence of a welfare state gives women more options than their traditional ones (depend on your father until marriage, then

L. Hamilton, *Welfare Doesn't Work*, Exploring the Basic Income Guarantee, https://doi.org/10.1007/978-3-030-37121-0_5

depend on your husband), which is threatening to our historical and cultural [read: patriarchal] preference for two-parent, male-headed, heterosexual families. A 1986 *Report of the White House Working Group on the Family* expressed fear that welfare "deprives men of their traditional role as providers" (Abramovitz, 1996, p. 269). Even today, teenage mothers are exempted from the TANF requirement to live with a guardian if they are married (Mink, 2006). Women who violate traditional social norms, have children outside of marriage, and then seek public assistance have been called "broodmares" (Joseph, 2006) and "welfare queens" by politicians, but there is relatively little discourse in welfare debates about the sexual activity or expectations of men (Piven & Cloward, 1993). Historically, welfare policies "almost invariably impose obligations on women as mothers that are not imposed on men" (Standing, 2017, p. 38).

A Woman's Place

The paternalistic relationship between American women and the state has existed since the country's founding. Early colonial social policies were designed within a context in which women were very much second-class citizens and had a clear "place" in society: the marital home. Women were expected to demonstrate the virtues of chastity and economy, and of course, submit to the male authorities in their lives. Women who violated these expectations faced harsh consequences. These social values are typified by Hester Primm's assignment to wear the letter "A" for adultery in *The Scarlet Letter*, a fictionalized account of actual colonial policies. While the physical labeling of recalcitrant women might have ended by the 1800s, early Charity Organization Societies (COS) reinforced sexual norms by advocating to commit women to reformatories if they gave birth to a second child outside of marriage (Abramovitz, 1996).

Such draconian policies may have evolved, but the underlying norms and expectations of women continued into the twentieth century. Mother's Pension applicants in the early 1900s were denied assistance if they conceived their children outside of marriage or if a woman left her husband (Jansson, 2014). Even after approval for a Mother's Pension, caseworkers would visit regularly to train women in proper cooking, cleaning, and sewing. When mothers were uncooperative with these visits or engaged in otherwise "immoral" behavior, they faced removal from the rolls (Abramovitz, 1996).

During the Great Depression, to reinforce the expectation that women's "rightful place" was in the home and caring for children, most married women were banned from jobs programs such as the Works Progress Administration (WPA). As a result, women held only 12% of WPA jobs (Abramovitz, 1996). When the economic stressors of the Depression caused increases in divorce and abandonment by husbands, Mother's Pension programs continued to deny aid to single mothers, with less than a tenth of female-headed households receiving assistance in 1934. These policies improved slightly as the Depression worsened, but continued to show a significant preference for women who had become primary breadwinners through the only socially acceptable means: widowhood. By 1939, nearly two-thirds of AFDC mothers were widowed, while only a quarter were divorced or separated (Abramovitz, 1996).

Aid to [Virtuous Women with] Dependent Children

When the national patchwork of Mother's Pension programs was replaced by Aid to Dependent Children (ADC; later Aid to Families with Dependent Children or AFDC), under the Social Security Act of 1935, the program continued to incentivize women's economic dependence on marriage. Monthly ADC payments ($18 for the first child and $12 for each additional child) were set well below other programs enacted in 1935 which primarily benefited men, including Old Age Assistance ($30 per person) and Unemployment Insurance (up to $85 per person) (Jansson, 2014). Mothers were not calculated into the household size for ADC/AFDC benefit levels until the 1950s (Jansson, 2014), and married couples were barred from the program. In 1961, the Social Security Act was amended for the first time to allow AFDC funds to households which included fathers, although few states took advantage of this option (Piven & Cloward, 1993).

Welfare rights organizers in the 1960s began protesting intrusive eligibility rules for AFDC that were absent from support aimed at men (unemployment and retirement programs). For example, "man-in-the-house" rules cut women off welfare if a man was caught in the home. To enforce these rules, workers often conducted "midnight raids" and "parked car surveillance" (Piven & Cloward, 1993, p. 127). One documented case included a worker climbing a tree at 2 AM to peer through the windows of an AFDC mother (Abramovitz, 1996). Most states, especially in the South, imposed "suitable home" rules, which meant that children living in "unsuitable" homes (usually involving the birth of children outside of marriage), could be denied aid entirely. For example, in 1959, Florida used its "suitable home" rule to expel 7000 families (containing 30,000 children, of which only 181 were actual cases of neglect or abuse) from its welfare rolls. More than 90% of the expelled families were black (Piven & Cloward, 1993). Some localities in the 1960s would press criminal "fornication" charges against mothers receiving welfare if caught with a man. A leader of the National Welfare Rights Organization, Johnnie Tillmon (1972), aptly described the relationship between women and AFDC as an abusive marriage.

> You trade in "a" man for "the" man. But you can't divorce him if he treats you bad. He can divorce you of course, cut you off anytime he wants. But in that case "he" keeps the kids, not you. "The" Man runs everything. In ordinary marriage, sex is supposed to be for your husband. On AFDC you're not supposed to have any sex at all. You give up control over your body. It's a condition of aid.... "The" man, the welfare system, controls your money. He tell you what to buy and what not to buy, where to buy it, and how much things cost. If things – rent, for instance – really costs more than he says they do, it's too bad for you.

Midnight raids and "man in the house" rules were finally overturned by the Supreme Court in 1967 and 1968, respectively (Abramovitz, 1996; Piven & Cloward, 1993). Simultaneously and somewhat ironically, contemporary politicians expressed concerns for declining marriage rates among African American households and blamed AFDC for making women less likely to marry. Whether intentionally or unintentionally, these concerns overlooked national economic trends and employment discrimination, in which African American men experienced much higher unemployment rates than their white counterparts and were therefore less able to support a family (Abramovitz, 1996).

Morality and Virtue

In the 1970s and '80s, a cultural and political backlash to the sexual revolution of the 1960s grew among evangelical Christians, typified by Jerry Falwell's Moral Majority (Jansson, 2014). This movement was extraordinarily effective in organizing Conservative voters around the issues of restricting abortion access, denying rights to LGBTQ citizens, and preventing a perceived “breakdown” of the two-parent, heterosexual family. These sentiments came to a boiling point in the early 1990s, when both Republicans and Democrats expressed significant concerns about growing rates of “illegitimacy.” In a now-famous 1993 op-ed, titled “The Coming White Underclass,” Charles Murray described the growth of nonmarital births among African Americans and resultant growth of “fatherless boys” as “*Lord of the Flies* writ large.” To this phenomenon, he ascribed “physical violence, immediate gratification, and predatory sex” (Murray, 1993) echoed three years later in Hillary Clinton’s now-infamous description of black, gang-involved youth as “super predators” (“Mrs. Clinton Campaign Speech,” 1996).

However, Murray described black illegitimacy rates as “old news.” His real concern was that white communities would begin to follow suit. He described illegitimacy as “the single most important social problem of our time – more important than crime, drugs, poverty, illiteracy, welfare or homelessness because it drives everything else” (Murray, 1993). Murray’s proposal to prevent all of these social problems was to end the AFDC program entirely and allow for “the natural forces that have done the job quite effectively for millennia,” by which he presumably meant the economic dependence of women on marriage/men.

Such proposals were at the forefront of the 1994 Congressional elections and Newt Gingrich’s *Contract with America*, which included policy proposals to cut welfare, slash taxes, create harsher penalties for crime, and increase funding for businesses and the military. The crescendo of these debates was the passage of the Personal Responsibility and Work Opportunity Reconciliation Act of 1996, which replaced AFDC with Temporary Assistance to Needy Families (TANF) and explicitly sought to end single motherhood. Bill Clinton and Conservatives in Congress both believed that the availability of AFDC incentivized nonmarital births. Arguably, they were observing cultural trends unrelated to social policy; by 1996, approximately 32% of all births occur outside of a married, heterosexual family (Child Trends, 2018).

While early welfare programs seemed conflicted about whether the intention of assistance was to allow (white) women to remain at home with their young children or push (black) women into the labor force, there is no longer any pretense about the employment expectations of recipient mothers. TANF requires single mothers to either work, volunteer, or be engaged in job training programs. This expectation, in part, reflects cultural shifts in women’s attachment to the labor force. However, married

TANF households are only expected to have one working spouse, meaning that married TANF mothers have the flexibility and choice of being a stay at home parent while single mothers do not (Mink, 2001).

In addition to work requirements, many scholars argue that TANF policy is no less intrusive into the sexual and reproductive lives of low-income women than it was in the era of midnight raids and "suitable home" rules. For example, single mothers can be denied benefits if they do not identify non-custodial fathers. Some states then pursue child support from fathers and keep the collected payments rather than passing them along to the mother (Cancian, Meyer, & Caspar, 2008). Women can also be denied assistance if they have additional children while receiving aid (Wallace, 2009).

Further, TANF offers financial incentives for states to provide abstinence-only education. The PRWORA explicitly requires such education to teach that "sexual activity outside of the context of marriage is likely to have harmful psychological and physical effects." This section of the law also emphasizes "the importance of attaining self-sufficiency before engaging in sexual activity" (Personal Responsibility and Work Opportunity Reconciliation Act, 1996). In other words, poor people shouldn't have sex. States have further financial incentives to engineer reproduction via an "illegitimacy reduction bonus" if they reduce statewide rates of nonmarital births and abortion (Mink, 2006).

In an era of increasing skepticism toward low-income, single women and their ability to parent, the Adoption and Safe Families Act of 1997 (passed a year after Welfare Reform) created state bonuses for increased adoptions and reduced the amount of time that families have to complete treatment plans before termination of parental rights (from 18 to 12 months). It did not, however, offer additional services for keeping families together (Mink, 2006). Going a step further, Utah considered legislation that would pay unmarried, pregnant women $3000 to surrender their babies for adoption (Abramovitz, 1996). With an inadequate social safety net, greater emphasis on adoption, and fewer services for family stability, low-income mothers are increasingly vulnerable to separation from their children. This cumulative policy shift (and the fact that affected families are disproportionately black) has been described as "Jane Crow." In 2018, the *New York Times* profiled one African American mother, Maisha, who put her five-year-old daughter, Deja, to bed one night and then took a bath with her headphones on. Deja came out of her room and, unable to find her mother, walked across the street to her grandmother's house. Maisha was arrested for child endangerment and Deja placed in foster care. While this would be a terrifying incident for any parent, it would likely be treated very differently in a middle-class, white neighborhood (Clifford & Silver-Greenberg, 2018).

The George W. Bush Administration also assumed that the solution to poverty was encouraging two people who were both experiencing the effects of wage depression and growing income inequality to enter into a legally binding economic dependency, diverting greater TANF funds into marriage promotion programs. Three prominent welfare researchers at the time argued that marriage promotion would not end poverty, but *would* allow significant grant funding to be funneled to private, religious organizations who offered the programs (Fineman, Mink, & Smith, 2003). Further, the explicit expectation that low-income women be married can leave women dependent on men and vulnerable to abuse. Indeed, domestic violence increases in TANF households immediately after the monthly payment as men attempt to gain control of the money (Hsu, 2017). In turn, women experiencing intimate partner violence are less likely to become economically self-sufficient (Thomas, Collier-Tenison, Maxwell, & Check, 2017).

When Washington legislators frame TANF policy to penalize single mothers, local welfare offices often reflect this tone in their interactions with families. Mothers applying for assistance face patronizing, subtly racist, and moralizing language from caseworkers. For example, researchers recorded and analyzed 232 interviews between caseworkers and applicants in three states (Masters, Lindhorst, & Meyers, 2014). Many included humiliating exchanges like the following.

- **Worker:** What's the father's name? **Client:** I can only think of his first name, that's ______. **Worker:** How long did you go out with him? **Client:** A while. But he's in denial. Only thing I can think of is his first name. **Worker:** If you went out with him awhile you should know his last name. […] Oh, I'm getting a message [from the computer]. I never got that before. […] I guess the system couldn't believe someone would only know the first name.
- **Worker:** Do you have your current ID? Are you getting child support? **Client:** Um, well right now, he's just helping me pay the mortgage so, I guess, yeah. **Worker:** Is he the father of all your children? **Client:** The other three, no, he's in prison, the father of the other three. **Worker:** You don't pick them good.

- **Worker:** How many children are in the home? **Client:** Five and one on the way. **Worker:** Why would you go ahead and do that? We can talk to y'all until we're blue in the face. You know you won't get any extra money.

Feminization of Poverty

While women represent roughly half of Supplemental Security Income and Unemployment Insurance recipients, they comprise 85% of adult TANF beneficiaries, because they are more likely to be single parents than men (Administration for Children and Families, 2019; Social Security Administration, 2019; US Department of Labor, 2019). This means that women are disproportionately affected by increasingly stringent TANF eligibility criteria, contributing to the so-called feminization of poverty and exacerbating the consequences of poverty for women and their children. While AFDC lifted 56% of children who would have otherwise been in deep poverty (incomes less than 50% of the poverty line) in 1995, TANF only lifted 18% of such children in 2014 (Center on Budget and Policy Priorities, 2018). Today, 17% of all US children live in poverty (Child Trends, 2019).

The feminization of poverty has significant repercussions for women, their children, and the entire economy. Poverty increases the risks of addiction and poor physical and mental health; as well as the likelihood of living in areas with environmental pollution. It also carries a life expectancy as much as 25% lower than the highest-income Americans (U.S. Government Accountability Office, 2007). Further, poverty is a more significant predictor of problem drinking in African Americans, suggesting that the intersectional pressures of poverty and racism leave black families especially vulnerable to poor health (Glass et al., 2017). Children living in poor households are "at greater risk for several negative outcomes such as poor academic achievement, school dropout, abuse and neglect, behavioral and socioemotional problems, physical health problems, and developmental delays" (American Psychological Association, n.d.). According to the non-partisan US Government Accountability Office (2007), the cumulative effects of poverty create lower overall workforce participation, higher crime, higher health costs, and ultimately, slows economic growth. Childhood poverty alone costs the United States $1.03 trillion per year (McLaughlin & Rank, 2018).

Arguably, attacks on single motherhood distract from the fact that women are paid less and therefore carry the burden of raising children with fewer resources than they equitably deserve. Women continue to experience a 19.5% wage gap with men in the United States (Institute for Women's Policy Research, 2019). Even in the same profession, women are paid less (I am intentionally not using the word "earn" here, as disparate pay is not an accurate representation of women's actual work effort.). For example, in my profession, social work, women are paid 93.6% of men's average pay. Female CEOs make 69.8% of male CEOs (Institute for Women's Policy Research, 2019). We also know that this disparity is widest for women of color. In 2018, black and Hispanic women were paid 65.3% and 61.6% of white male wages, respectively (Hegewisch & Hartmann, 2019). Ultimately, the wage gap means that women are much more likely to be paid less than the federal poverty measurement (Institute for Women's Policy Research, 2019). Eight percent of working-age American men lived in poverty in 2017 compared to 11% of adult women, a difference of 2.5 million more women than men (Henry J. Kaiser Family Foundation, 2018).

Meanwhile, full-time, center-based child care in the United States averages $1230 per month, and home-based care is roughly $800 per month (Workman & Jessen-Howard, 2018). By comparison, the median monthly income for households in the lowest and second-lowest quintiles were $1104 and $2723 in 2017, respectively (US Census Bureau, 2018). The average monthly earnings for a full-time minimum-wage worker is $1256 (UC Davis Center for Poverty Research, 2018), calling into question whether it is even cost-effective to push low-income women with young children into the workforce before they have gained sufficient skills to improve their income potential. Under TANF rules, however, vocational training and education only count toward work requirements for 12 months (Black & Sprague, 2017), making it difficult to earn anything more than a GED or certificate in fields that arguably, continue to pay sub-sufficiency incomes. This policy shift may explain why the pre-1996 AFDC program was more effective in moving recipients with less than a high school diploma to the workforce than TANF, as recipients had more time to complete a GED and gain further job training (Cancian, Meyer, & Wu, 2005).

Basic-Income Outcomes for Women

Some progressive feminists argue that a universal basic income is the best way to truly create equal opportunities for women in society (Zelleke, 2011). Firstly, it can protect women from exploitation and domestic violence when they are not financially dependent on men or when a small welfare check creates a power imbalance in an economically strained household. A review of 165 basic income studies discovered lower fertility, delayed marriage, decreased sexual assault among women, and better school attendance for girls (Hagen-Zanker et al., 2016). One pilot of 1000 people in Namibia found that female recipients gained greater economic independence and were less likely to engage in prostitution (Haarmann et al., 2008).

However, the relationship between mothers and employment continues to be a political hurdle for basic income advocates. Women in the 1970s Mincome experiment expressed gratitude that the pilot allowed them to care for young children (Calnitsky, 2016), but the idea that women should receive government support to stay at home with children is controversial in modern American politics on both sides of the aisle. Conservatives are uncomfortable with government support for anyone who is not actively seeking work and liberals chafe at any implication that a mother's "rightful" place is at home, especially when there are no adverse outcomes associated with high-quality child care in comparison to children who remain with a stay at home parent (Oster, 2019).

The advantage of basic income is that it allows women and their families to make the marriage, fertility, and child care decisions that are right for *them*; no paternalistic social engineering or intrusive eligibility criteria required. If a woman chooses to remain at home while her children are young or to leave a violent relationship, a basic income allows for that. If a mother elects to return to the workforce, a basic income can help with child care expenses or provide an income floor in the event of unreliable employment. Just a few months after the pilot launched, a single mother of two in the modern Stockton, California demonstration told reporters that she would continue working two jobs to support her children, but that the $500 basic income support had significantly reduced her level of stress (Meza, 2019).

Finally, basic-income advocates argue that it would more fairly compensate women for millions of hours of unpaid labor contributed to household tasks, child care, and elder care performed each year. For example, American women provide 69% of unpaid caregiving for senior members of the family (Johnson & Wiener, 2016). If the deficit between American men's and women's household labor were monetized, the average women would receive an additional $7300 per year (Merelli & Zhou, 2018). Globally, women contribute 2.6 times the amount of household work of men and a total of $28 trillion in annual, unpaid global productivity (Berman, 2018). As Guy Standing, a founder of the Basic Income Earth Network, argues, "traditionally, men have been free-riders on unpaid domestic work done mostly by women. A basic income would be justified to compensate for this work" (Standing, 2017, p. 170).

References

Abramovitz, M. (1996). *Regulating the Lives of Women: Social Welfare Policy from Colonial Times to the Present.* Boston: South End Press.

Administration for Children and Families. (2019). *Characteristics and Financial Circumstances of TANF Recipients, Fiscal Year 2018.* Retrieved November 6, 2019, from Office of Family Assistance | ACF Website: https://www.acf.hhs.gov/ofa/resource/characteristics-and-financial-circumstances-of-tanf-recipients-fiscal-year-2018

American Psychological Association. (n.d.). *Effects of Poverty, Hunger and Homelessness on Children and Youth.* Retrieved May 23, 2019, from https://www.apa.org Website: https://www.apa.org/pi/families/poverty

Berman, J. (2018). *Women's Unpaid Work Is the Backbone of the American Economy.* Retrieved October 25, 2018, from Market Watch Website: https://www.marketwatch.com/story/this-is-how-much-more-unpaid-work-women-do-than-men-2017-03-07

Black, R., & Sprague, A. (2017). *Becoming Visible: Race, Economic Security, and Political Voice in Jackson, Mississippi.* Retrieved from New America Foundation Website: https://www.newamerica.org/family-centered-social-policy/policy-papers/becoming-visible/

Calnitsky, D. (2016). "More Normal than Welfare": The Mincome Experiment, Stigma, and Community Experience. *Canadian Review of Sociology/Revue Canadienne de Sociologie, 53*(1), 26–71. https://doi.org/10.1111/cars.12091.

Cancian, M., Meyer, D. R., & Caspar, E. (2008). Welfare and Child Support: Complements, Not Substitutes. *Journal of Policy Analysis and Management, 27*(2), 354–375.

Cancian, M., Meyer, D. R., & Wu, C.-F. (2005). After the Revolution: Welfare Patterns Since TANF Implementation. *Social Work Research, 29*(4), 199–214. https://doi.org/10.1093/swr/29.4.199.

Center on Budget and Policy Priorities. (2018). *TANF Lifts Many Fewer Children out of Deep Poverty than AFDC Did*. Retrieved from Center for Budget Policies and Priorities Website: https://www.cbpp.org/tanf-lifts-many-fewer-children-out-of-deep-poverty-than-afdc-did-7

Child Trends. (2018). *Births to Unmarried Women*. Retrieved from Child Trends Website: https://www.childtrends.org/indicators/births-to-unmarried-women

Child Trends. (2019). *Children in Poverty*. Retrieved May 23, 2019, from https://www.childtrends.org/indicators/children-in-poverty

Clifford, S., & Silver-Greenberg, J. (2018, January 20). Foster Care as Punishment: The New Reality of 'Jane Crow.' *The New York Times*. Retrieved from https://www.nytimes.com/2017/07/21/nyregion/foster-care-nyc-jane-crow.html

Fineman, M., Mink, G., & Smith, A. M. (2003). No Promotion of Marriage in TANF. *Social Justice, 30*(4), 126–134.

Glass, J. E., Rathouz, P. J., Gattis, M., Joo, Y. S., Nelson, J. C., & Williams, E. C. (2017). Intersections of Poverty, Race/Ethnicity, and Sex: Alcohol Consumption and Adverse Outcomes in the United States. *Social Psychiatry and Psychiatric Epidemiology, 52*(5), 515–524. https://doi.org/10.1007/s00127-017-1362-4.

Haarmann, C., Haarmann, D., Jauch, H., Shindonola-Mote, H., Nattrass, N., Samson, M., & Standing, G. (2008). *Towards a Basic Income Grant for All: Basic Income Grant Pilot Project Assessment Report, September 2008*. Retrieved from NANGOF Website: http://www.bignam.org/Publications/BIG_Assessment_report_08a.pdf

Hagen-Zanker, J., Bastagli, F., Harman, L., Barca, V., Sturge, G., & Schmidt, T. (2016). *Understanding the Impact of Cash Transfers: The Evidence*. London: Overseas Development Institute.

Hegewisch, A., & Hartmann, H. (2019). *The Gender Wage Gap: 2018 Earnings Differences by Race and Ethnicity* (No. C478). Retrieved from Institute for Women's Policy Research Website: https://iwpr.org/publications/gender-wage-gap-2018/

Henry J. Kaiser Family Foundation. (2018). *Nonelderly Adult Poverty Rate by Gender*. Retrieved from Henry J. Kaiser Family Foundation Website: https://www.kff.org/other/state-indicator/adult-poverty-rate-by-gender/

Hsu, L.-C. (2017). The Timing of Welfare Payments and Intimate Partner Violence. *Economic Inquiry, 55*(2), 1017–1031. https://doi.org/10.1111/ecin.12413.

Institute for Women's Policy Research. (2019). *Pay Equity & Discrimination*. Retrieved May 23, 2019, from Institute for Women's Policy Research Website: https://iwpr.org/issue/employment-education-economic-change/pay-equity-discrimination/

Jansson, B. S. (2014). *The Reluctant Welfare State: Engaging History to Advance Social Work Practice in Contemporary Society* (8th ed.). Belmont, CA: Cengage Learning.

Johnson, R. W., & Wiener, J. M. (2016, June 4). *A Profile of Frail Older Americans and Their Caregivers*. Retrieved May 23, 2019, from Urban Institute Website: https://www.urban.org/research/publication/profile-frail-older-americans-and-their-caregivers

Joseph, A. (2006). Welfare Reform: Forward to the Past. In K. Kilty & E. Segal (Eds.), *The Promise of Welfare Reform: Political Rhetoric and Reality of Poverty in the Twenty-First Century* (pp. 39–47). New York: Hawthorne.

Masters, N. T., Lindhorst, T. P., & Meyers, M. K. (2014). Jezebel at the Welfare Office: How Racialized Stereotypes of Poor Women's Reproductive Decisions and Relationships Shape Policy Implementation. *Journal of Poverty, 18*(2), 109–129. https://doi.org/10.1080/10875549.2013.833159.

McLaughlin, M., & Rank, M. R. (2018). Estimating the Economic Cost of Childhood Poverty in the United States. *Social Work Research, 42*(2), 73–83. https://doi.org/10.1093/swr/svy007.

Merelli, A., & Zhou, Y. (2018). *This Calculator Puts a Dollar Value on the Unpaid Work Done by Women*. Retrieved October 25, 2018, from Quartz at Work Website: https://qz.com/work/1083411/this-calculator-makes-the-unpaid-work-women-do-visible/

Meza, M. (2019, May 23). *Stockton Woman Says Guaranteed Income Program Has Been Life-Changing*. Retrieved May 24, 2019, from KCRA Website: https://www.kcra.com/article/stockton-woman-says-guaranteed-income-program-has-been-life-changing/27564001

Mink, G. (2001). Violating Women: Rights Abuses in the Welfare Police State. *The Annals of the American Academy of Political and Social Science, 577*, 79–93.

Mink, G. (2006). Ending Single Motherhood. In K. Kilty & E. Segal (Eds.), *The Promise of Welfare Reform: Political Rhetoric and Reality of Poverty in the Twenty-First Century* (pp. 155–168). New York: Hawthorne.

Mrs. Clinton Campaign Speech. (1996, January 25). Retrieved July 29, 2019, from CSPAN Website: https://www.c-span.org/video/?c4558907/mrs-clinton-campaign-speech-super-predators

Murray, C. (1993, October 29). The Coming White Underclass. *Wall Street Journal*. Retrieved from http://www.aei.org/publication/the-coming-white-underclass/

Oster, E. (2019). *Cribsheet: A Data-Driven Guide to Better, More Relaxed Parenting, from Birth to Preschool*. London: Penguin.

Personal Responsibility and Work Opportunity Reconciliation Act of 1996. Pub. L. No. 104–193, 42 601 42 USC 601 (1996).

Piven, F. F., & Cloward, R. (1993). *Regulating the Poor: The Functions of Public Welfare* (Updated, Subsequent ed.). New York: Vintage.

Social Security Administration. (2019). *Fast Facts & Figures About Social Security, 2019.* Retrieved November 6, 2019, from Social Security Administration Research, Statistics, and Policy Analysis Website: https://www.ssa.gov/policy/docs/chartbooks/fast_facts/2019/fast_facts19.html

Standing, G. (2017). *Basic Income: A Guide for the Open-Minded.* New Haven, CT/London: Yale University Press.

Thomas, J., Collier-Tenison, S., Maxwell, D., & Check, C. (2017). TANF Participation and Intimate Partner Violence: Exploring Barriers to Self-Sufficiency. *International Journal of Social Science Studies, 5*, 20–31.

Tillmon, J. (1972). Welfare Is a Woman's Issue. *Ms. Magazine.* Retrieved from https://www.rapereliefshelter.bc.ca/learn/resources/welfare-womens-issue-johnnie-tillmon

U.S. Government Accountability Office. (2007). *Poverty in America: Consequences for Individuals and the Economy.* Retrieved from https://www.gao.gov/products/GAO-07-343T

UC Davis Center for Poverty Research. (2018, January 12). *What Are the Annual Earnings for a Full-Time Minimum Wage Worker?* Retrieved May 23, 2019, from UC Davis Center for Poverty Research Website: https://poverty.ucdavis.edu/faq/what-are-annual-earnings-full-time-minimum-wage-worker

US Census Bureau. (2018, August 28). *Historical Income Tables: Households.* Retrieved May 23, 2019, from https://www.census.gov/data/tables/time-series/demo/income-poverty/historical-income-households.html

US Department of Labor. (2019). *September 2019 Characteristics of Unemployment Insurance Claimants.* Retrieved November 6, 2019, from https://oui.doleta.gov/unemploy/content/chariu2019/2019Sep.html

Wallace, G. L. (2009). The Effects of Family Caps on the Subsequent Fertility Decisions of Never-Married Mothers. *Journal of Population Research, 26*(1), 73–101.

Workman, S., & Jessen-Howard, S. (2018, November 15). *Understanding the True Cost of Child Care for Infants and Toddlers.* Retrieved May 23, 2019, from Center for American Progress Website: https://www.americanprogress.org/issues/early-childhood/reports/2018/11/15/460970/understanding-true-cost-child-care-infants-toddlers/

Zelleke, A. (2011). Feminist Political Theory and the Argument for an Unconditional Basic Income. *Policy & Politics, 39*(1), 27–42. https://doi.org/10.1332/030557311X546299.

CHAPTER 6

A Two-Tiered Welfare State

Abstract The eligibility rules, sanctions, and privacy intrusions discussed in previous chapters only exist in programs aimed at low-income families. None of these features can be found in programs aimed at middle- or upper-income families, which constitute much greater proportions of the total federal budget. Possible explanations for this double standard include the application of ascetic values to needy families and lower levels of empathy across racial groups. The two tiers of social policy have detrimental effects to all Americans. Basic-income advocates argue that the only way to address unfair social policy is to replace significant pieces of it with one, universal system.

Keywords Welfare • Taxes • Asceticism • Race • Empathy • Democracy

Adam Smith, the father of modern economics, argued that when a person acts to maximize his financial gain, the entire economy benefits. If a person builds wealth, for example, they can invest in a business, education, homeownership, or the stock market, in turn, contributing to overall economic growth. The United States has built an entire tax code on this notion. We want people to buy a home and save for retirement, so we make mortgage interest and 401k contributions tax-deductible. This logic is reversed, however, when designing systems for low-income citizens.

L. Hamilton, *Welfare Doesn't Work*, Exploring the Basic Income Guarantee, https://doi.org/10.1007/978-3-030-37121-0_6

The strict eligibility rules, sanctions, and privacy intrusions discussed in previous chapters only exist in programs aimed at low-income families because we believe that the poor should be discouraged from maximizing personal gain in government programs. The two tiers of American social policy created by this double standard have significant effects for both economically marginalized households and society in general.

Welfare Expenditures by Social Class

Three of the primary social expenditures aimed at middle- and upper-income households include relatively low capital gains taxes, tax-sheltered retirement accounts, and the mortgage interest deduction (MID), which cost the government \$134.6, \$82.7, and \$77 billion in 2016, respectively (DeSilver, 2016). While the capital gains tax is somewhat complicated and depends on how long you hold an asset, the general idea is that the growth of assets (e.g. property or other investments) are taxed at a lower rate than employment income. Depending on your level of income, capital gains are taxed between zero and 20%, while employment income is capped at 37% (Tax Policy Center, 2018). This difference is especially beneficial to wealthy Americans, who often earn more revenue from investments than employment.

Popular among homeowners (especially owners of multiple homes), the MID is controversial among economists. In an article titled "*Why Economists Don't Like the Mortgage Interest Deduction*," a writer for the Federal Reserve Bank of St. Louis explains that the MID incentivizes buyers to purchase larger houses than they might otherwise, knowing that interest paid on the loan can be deducted from their annual tax liability (Smith, 2018). Families buying bigger houses increases national home energy consumption and urban sprawl. Because people are more likely to buy bigger homes, they are also more likely to default on their loan. Further, as middle- and upper-income households are encouraged to buy bigger houses, real estate values are inflated, putting homeownership out of reach for lower-income families and actually *reducing* the overall homeownership rate. If eliminated, research suggests that homeownership would increase by 5% and the average mortgage balance would go down by 30% (Smith, 2018). Though the MID is theoretically structured to encourage homeownership across income levels, it ultimately functions as a direct subsidy to upper-income households, with 90% of the benefit going to households making more than $100,000 per year (Thompson, 2017).

Altogether, the IRS Code included more than $1.3 trillion in annual tax breaks in 2016 (DeSilver, 2016). Further, corporate tax rates have been declining in comparison to household taxes for decades (National Priorities Project, 2019). A new tax law in 2017 included an *additional* $1.3 trillion in corporate tax breaks over ten years (or $130 billion per year), 70% of which will go directly into the pockets of the top 20% of income earners (Center on Budget and Policy Priorities, 2018a). Meanwhile, programs aimed at the poor constitute relatively smaller portions of the total federal budget. The TANF program, for example, has been budgeted at $16.5 billion every year since 1996 (Center on Budget and Policy Priorities, 2015). The annual budgets for SNAP and SSI are $70 billion and $59 billion, respectively (Center on Budget and Policy Priorities, 2018b, 2018c). Overall, all low-income social programs (including TANF, SNAP, SSI, the refundable EITC and Child Tax Credit, low-income housing assistance, the free school breakfast and lunch programs, childcare subsidies, low-income heating assistance, and child welfare intervention services) constituted only 9% (or $357 billion) of the total federal budget in 2017 (Center on Budget and Policy Priorities, 2019a).

Bureaucratic Hurdles and Administrative Cost

Though poverty programs constitute a relatively small share of the total government budget, applicants have historically faced significant bureaucratic hurdles, which are unseen in programs more frequently used by middle- and upper-income households. In the 1960s, for example, mothers receiving AFDC were required to answer questions about their sexual activity and menstruation, and have their homes inspected for any sign of a man's presence. Multiple legal challenges to these practices were unsuccessful, with the courts determining that welfare applicants waive their constitutional rights to privacy (Piven & Cloward, 1993). These rules were eventually overturned, but applying for welfare continues to be a burdensome and intrusive process.

Today, needy families face a lengthy eligibility determination process (which is reauthorized at regular intervals), often requiring birth certificates, tax returns, pay stubs, proof of any asset holdings, and submission to intrusive, dehumanizing interviews. A mother speaking of her experiences with her local welfare office told researchers that "it seems like they look at us like we're beneath them because we need the help. And then they talk to us in a kind of way. No one wants to go through that" (Black & Sprague, 2017). Another mother in the same study described the experience of waiting hours to be seen by welfare caseworkers.

> [After work] you got to go to the welfare office, the social security office, these places that are there to help you, and you go there and you're already tired, you're already frustrated, you've already been sitting there 3–4 hours before you're even being seen, and then you finally get up to a person and all they got for you is attitude [...] then the next time you gotta come you don't even want to come. (Black & Sprague, 2017)

One MTurker described their experience with SNAP offices as follows: "Sometimes the people who are supposed to be helping you are very rude and condescending because you need help."

Further, many recipients explain that the disorganization of welfare offices means having to produce the same documentation repeatedly or else risk losing benefits.

> After numerous experiences supplying duplicative paperwork to apply and recertify for programs, 'Tracee' applied her characteristically methodical troubleshooting skills and began keeping a stack of her family's birth certificates handy so she could just grab them when needed. Ultimately, though, she was investing time and energy in a system designed to devalue both. 'Well, when I went to recertify, I gave the lady all my stuff that she asked me for. And I asked her did she need anything else. She was like, 'No, Miss C, I don't need anything else. That's it.' So I didn't receive my SNAP benefits on my card, and I called and asked why. She was like, 'Well, you didn't bring me what I told you to bring me.' And I was like, 'Remember, I came to your office.' She denied everything because she didn't want to get in trouble with her supervisor. And I don't know what happened to my papers or whatever, but I just don't like going in there at all because it's always something.' (Black & Sprague, 2017)

An MTurker and former SNAP recipient told me, "The overall experience was really stressful and complicated at times like when filling out the application online, renewing, or reporting changes. When having to call your caseworker I would never get a response the same day it was always a day or so later and even then, the issue would not be resolved." While these examples are anecdotal, it is difficult to conjure similar cases when middle-income families deduct their mortgage interest from annual tax filings or sign up for their employers' 401k plan.

Even in Canada, recipients of social assistance report intrusive eligibility rules. One basic-income recipient in Ontario explained that when she received traditional assistance,

> There [were] too many rules. Just if, like I had a roommate J*** actually, we were roommates. They gave me a thing I had to fill out. J*** was on assistance too but he didn't have to, I did. Want to know about our relationship; did we have any kids together? Did we share the same room? Were we intimate? Very intrusive stuff like that. Even though we weren't, like I had no problem answering, it's just very intrusive, very personal information that they want. Which I don't think is really any of their business. (Hamilton & Mulvale, 2019, p. 591)

These bureaucratic hurdles can be so time-consuming that they interfere in a recipient's ability to move toward independence. One MTurker, a former recipient of TANF and SNAP, explained, "The check-ins and reporting requirements were sometimes in the way of actually finding work or expanding my educational opportunities."

The eligibility determination process ostensibly serves to ensure that only the truly needy receive assistance, but has the unintended (or possibly intended?) consequence of deterring a great number of needy applicants from even applying. It also comes with a significant administrative price tag. Workers must spend considerable time conducting intake interviews, processing applicant paperwork, and recertifying current recipients. Of the total TANF budget, for example, 11% is spent on administration, compared to less than 1% of the Old Age, Survivors and Disability Insurance program (more commonly known as Social Security) budget (Schott & Floyd, 2017; Social Security Administration, 2019). This difference is because Social Security is a universal program: everyone is eligible once they reach a certain age, so no caseworkers are needed to investigate applicants or reauthorize their eligibility regularly. For this reason, basic-income advocates have long argued that universal programs, like Social Security, are more effective at addressing poverty and simultaneously come with significantly lower administration costs (Bell & Bushe, 1975; Hamilton & Martin-West, 2019). "Without Social Security benefits, 39.2 percent of elderly Americans would have incomes below the official poverty line, all else being equal; with Social Security benefits, only

9.2 percent do," making it the most effective and efficient anti-poverty program in the United States (Center on Budget and Policy Priorities, 2019b).

Morality and Class

Middle- and upper-income citizens have little qualm with taking full advantage of the policy expenditures available to them. Indeed, a high earner is considered foolish if they do not hire an accountant to secure every possible tax break for which they are eligible. However, a stigma exists for low-income people who similarly take advantage of programs available to them. As two MTurkers explained, "Getting Food Stamps helped me get by during some rough times. However, it is a little embarrassing to have to rely on the help to buy food to live on" and "There are all sorts of social stigmas around governmental aid. It is a bit embarrassing."

The question then becomes, why do we have different sets of expectations for low- and middle-income populations, especially when poverty programs make up such a relatively small portion of the total federal budget? The first possible explanation is the dominant American cultural (i.e., Protestant Christian) application of ascetic values to those living in poverty. Asceticism is the idea that one gains spiritually and morally by living simply and denying oneself small pleasures. Dating to the Greeks, asceticism was historically a way for the pious—monks, mystics, and the like—to gain a nearly transcendental experience. Only in more recent, western history have ascetic principles been folded into the Protestant values of hard work and simple living and applied to the general population (Arnold, 2005).

Political philosopher Kathleen Arnold (2005) argues that ascetic principles have now been twisted in modern social policy as a way to punish the poor for their presumed excesses and lack of self-control. Regulations on the reproduction of welfare applicants and expectation that they take any work offered (even if that work offers sub-poverty level wages or exploitative conditions) are seen as necessary to instill self-discipline in the poor. We see additional examples of this narrative in modern welfare discourse when middle-class Americans opine that the ownership of TVs or microwaves and vices such as cigarettes and junk food ought to disqualify the poor from receiving assistance.

It is important to note that this mainstream expectation does not exist for CEOs accepting corporate welfare or middle-class citizens receiving the substantial tax breaks described earlier. Keep in mind that the average mortgage interest deduction can reach $6365 in areas with high real estate values, while the average TANF grant is $450 monthly or $5400 annually (Burnside & Floyd, 2019; Li, 2017). Also, homeowners can apply for this deduction every year for the life of their mortgage, while TANF recipients are limited to a lifetime maximum of five years, so the cumulative difference is substantial. This double standard exists because the intertwining of capitalist and ascetic values in modern American society means that, according to the dominant narrative, those with material wealth (whether earned or inherited) have proven themselves as worthy citizens and do not require outwardly imposed discipline.

Further, ascetic expectations of the poor, especially a devotion to hard and low-paid work has been an effective tool to discourage unionization and ensure a ready supply of cheap labor for the difficult, but necessary tasks of capitalism. My three-year-old son was recently gifted a book by his preschool teachers, entitled *Animal Strike at the Zoo*, in which zoo animals go on strike because they are "paid only peanuts," fed only hay, and lack a series of increasingly preposterous demands such as swimming pools and ice cream (Wilson, 2006). The strike resolves when a little girl comes to the zoo and begins to cry because the animals are not performing. "No birdies are peeping. No lizards are creeping. No bunnies are leaping." The animals realize the error of their ways, drop the strike, and begin performing their duties again. While a silly example, the moral of this Marxist-dystopia-come-children's-book is that if all workers realized the value of their work—making children happy in this instance—they would not make ridiculous demands like fair pay and good working conditions.

Empathy and Race

A second possible explanation for the two tiers of expectations placed on welfare recipients and beneficiaries of other government expenditures is the human ability to feel empathy for people who are different from us. Because welfare recipients are stereotypically non-white, research on cross-racial empathy provides important insights. In lab experiments, people show more empathy for people of their own race than people of other races. For example, one oft-repeated experiment includes showing participants a needle piercing a hand with various skin tones. The areas of the brain associated with empathy are more likely to be triggered if the hand belongs to someone of the same race as the participant (Chiao & Mathur, 2010). This finding is true for people of all races, but the fact that white people are better able to sympathize with other white people is significant when considering that whites make up nearly 73% of voters, 78% of Congress, and more than 80% of State Legislators (Ballotpedia, 2019; National Conference of State Legislatures, 2015; Pew Research Center, 2019).

The dynamics of race and empathy play out in multiple areas of government. For example, it is well documented that the race of jurors, victims, and defendants play a complex role in the outcome of criminal trials. If a white jury is faced with a white victim and a black defendant, they are more likely to render a guilty verdict. Conversely, when faced with a white defendant, white jurors are more likely to be lenient (Linder, 1995).

Put simply, white Americans, who are statistically more likely to be making decisions about welfare policy—either as voters or as politicians—have less empathy for the plight of racial minorities in poverty. While African Americans make up less than 25% of means-tested public assistance recipients (Foster & Rojas, 2018), the dominant belief that they are the primary beneficiaries combined with lower empathy for those outside one's own race carries significant repercussions for public support of welfare programs. In surveys, one of the strongest predictors for supporting punitive welfare policy is the presence of stereotyped beliefs about racial minorities, such as the belief that "Blacks are lazy" (Limbert & Bullock, 2005).

These unconscious dynamics are easily exploited by legislators seeking to cut funding for social programs by conjuring race-based stereotypes, as Reagan did when speaking of the "Welfare Queen in Chicago." In one experiment, college students who were exposed to images of African Americans looting after Hurricane Katrina were less likely to agree with statements of policy and financial support for African American hurricane victims, although their support for white victims remained unchanged. Similar results were found when participants were "primed" with exposure to rap music that sexualized African American women: White respondents expressed less empathy and policy support toward young black mothers (Johnson, Olivo, Gibson, Reed, & Ashburn-Nardo, 2009). Critical race theorists argue that politicians knowingly employ these stereotypes as an effective tool to divide citizens by race and class in order to distract the political narrative from declining wages and increasing inequality (Limbert & Bullock, 2005).

Welfare and Democracy

The divisions between welfare beneficiaries and "everyone else" carries potential ramifications for American democracy and civic life. As late as the 1960s, AFDC recipients received routine threats that they would lose their benefits if they engaged in any political activity that went against the state's best interest (protests, filing complaints of discrimination, or even voting) (Piven & Cloward, 1993). These tactics are no longer in practice, but significant research suggests that receiving assistance from means-tested programs still decreases the likelihood to vote or engage in one's community (volunteering, belonging to clubs, etc.), while universal programs like Social Security have the opposite effect (Black & Sprague, 2017; Campbell, 2011).

Of course, multiple factors contribute to this gap. Firstly, Social Security recipients are older than beneficiaries of other programs and therefore, statistically more likely to vote (Misra, 2019). Further, by definition, Social Security beneficiaries are less likely to work or have other pressing demands on their time like parenting small children, and therefore, hypothetically have more time to engage. Meanwhile, financial benefits in other programs are usually lower, so recipients are often working multiple jobs and have less time to get to the polls or volunteer in their communities. However, differences in age, time, and work status do not completely explain the civic engagement gap between public programs.

Harsh eligibility criteria and negative experiences with welfare offices are specifically associated with lower voter turnout and civic engagement. The more punitive a state's welfare system is the more likely low-income voters are to be disengaged (Bruch, Ferree, & Soss, 2010). The TANF program, especially, has more negative consequences for engagement compared to less harsh programs like Head Start (Bruch et al., 2010). The dehumanizing experience of interacting with welfare offices, as described by several recipients mentioned earlier, very likely increase negative feelings toward American government, civic life, and the political system, which, in turn, creates disengagement.

This disenfranchisement is dangerous to American democracy—only 56% of voting-age adults cast ballots in 2016, a rate significantly lower than most industrialized democracies (DeSilver, 2018). When fewer people vote, politicians must craft their message toward "likely voters," or people who feel passionately about politics and their political positions. These voters tend to more extreme than average Americans, and political commentators have argued that low turnout by moderate, less-engaged voters has pushed political rhetoric and, importantly, social policy toward polarization (Rettig, 2010). These observers argue that increasing turnout among all Americans is a critical component to ending current political gridlock.

Equality Through a Basic Income

One primary function of a UBI scheme is to eliminate the two tiers of society created by double standards in public programs. According to Guy Standing, a long-time leader in the basic income movement, effective and humane social policy must pass two important principles. First, the "Paternalism Test Principle" states that "a social policy is unjust if it imposes controls on some groups that are not imposed on the most free groups in society." Secondly, the "Rights-not-Charity Principle" states, "A social policy is just only if it advances the rights or freedom of the recipient or target person rather than the discretion or power of the provider" (Standing, 2017).

In other words, social policy is just when it treats every citizen equally and humanely. We cannot be a united American people when social policy continues to separate us into the 400-year-old categories of "deserving" and "undeserving." The argument that low-income families must not "leach off" the government falls flat when middle- and upper-income citizens gain just as much (or more) financially without having to submit to paternalistic and dehumanizing eligibility criteria. It is easy to imagine the uproar if Americans were suddenly ineligible for mortgage interest deductions after having a third or fourth child or if CEOs were required to submit to a drug test before their corporation could accept tax incentives.

Early data suggest that basic income has the potential to remove these artificial delineations. Many pilot recipients in Ontario reported the feeling of freedom gained by basic income as compared to their previous experiences with traditional public assistance. They were no longer spending time proving that they were worthy of aid or interacting with condescending caseworkers. One recipient explained the revolutionary effects that this change had on their life and outlook.

> Basic income changed my life. I also know people whose lives were changed for the better.…Not having to visit the ODSP office [Ontario's disability

> insurance program] every month and have a worker be paid to manage my 'case' was great. Having someone to call at BIP [Basic Income Pilot] only when I had a question was great. Not dealing with the stigma of being on ODSP brought dignity to my life. (Basic Income Canada Network, 2019)

Elegantly, another recipient stated that they "finally felt like a part of society" (Basic Income Canada Network, 2019).

References

Arnold, K. R. (2005). Asceticism in Contemporary Political Theory: Marx, Weber, Nietzsche and Beyond. *Theory & Event, 8*(2). https://doi.org/10.1353/tae.2005.0019.

Ballotpedia. (2019). *116th United States Congress*. Retrieved June 26, 2019, from Ballotpedia Website: https://ballotpedia.org/116th_United_States_Congress

Basic Income Canada Network. (2019). *Signposts to Success: Report of a BICN Survey of Ontario Basic Income Recipients*. Retrieved from Basic Income Canada Network Website: https://www.basicincomecanada.org/time_for_national_action_new_report_shows_ontario_basic_income_pilot_was_on_track_to_success?fbclid=IwAR1BcwCr6pQ-kLHv_YRXddbK48jv2OLH9pGX-X1rU_946RB-Kvro2wvVrCg

Bell, W., & Bushe, D. M. (1975). *The Economic Efficiency of AFDC. Social Service Review, 49*(2), 175–190.

Black, R., & Sprague, A. (2017). *Becoming Visible: Race, Economic Security, and Political Voice in Jackson, Mississippi*. Retrieved from New America Foundation Website: https://www.newamerica.org/family-centered-social-policy/policy-papers/becoming-visible/

Bruch, S. K., Ferree, M. M., & Soss, J. (2010). From Policy to Polity: Democracy, Paternalism, and the Incorporation of Disadvantaged Citizens. *American Sociological Review, 75*(2), 205–226. https://doi.org/10.1177/0003122410363563.

Burnside, A., & Floyd, I. (2019). *TANF Benefits Remain Low Despite Recent Increases in Some States*. Retrieved from Center on Budget Policies and Priorities Website: https://www.cbpp.org/research/family-income-support/tanf-benefits-remain-low-despite-recent-increases-in-some-states

Campbell, A. L. (2011). *How Policies Make Citizens: Senior Political Activism and the American Welfare State*. Princeton, NJ: Princeton University Press.

Center on Budget and Policy Priorities. (2015). Policy Basics: An Introduction to TANF. Retrieved July 19, 2017, from Center on Budget and Policy Priorities Website: https://www.cbpp.org/research/policy-basics-an-introduction-to-tanf

Center on Budget and Policy Priorities. (2018a). *Corporate Tax Cut Benefits Wealthiest, Loses Needed Revenue, and Encourages Tax Avoidance*. Retrieved from Center on Budget Policies and Priorities Website: https://www.cbpp.

org/research/federal-tax/corporate-tax-cut-benefits-wealthiest-loses-needed-revenue-and-encourages-tax

Center on Budget and Policy Priorities. (2018b). Policy Basics: Supplemental Security Income. Retrieved March 21, 2019, from Center on Budget and Policy Priorities Website: https://www.cbpp.org/research/social-security/policy-basics-supplemental-security-income

Center on Budget and Policy Priorities. (2018c). *Policy Basics: The Supplemental Nutrition Assistance Program (SNAP)*. Retrieved from Center on Budget Policies and Priorities Website: https://www.cbpp.org/research/policy-basics-the-supplemental-nutrition-assistance-program-snap

Center on Budget and Policy Priorities. (2019a). *Policy Basics: Where Do Our Federal Tax Dollars Go?* Retrieved from Center for Budget Policies and Priorities Website: https://www.cbpp.org/research/federal-budget/policy-basics-where-do-our-federal-tax-dollars-go

Center on Budget and Policy Priorities. (2019b). *Social Security Lifts More Americans Above Poverty than Any Other Program*. Retrieved from https://www.cbpp.org/research/social-security/social-security-lifts-more-americans-above-poverty-than-any-other-program

Chiao, J. Y., & Mathur, V. A. (2010). Intergroup Empathy: How Does Race Affect Empathic Neural Responses? *Current Biology, 20*(11), R478–R480. https://doi.org/10.1016/j.cub.2010.04.001.

DeSilver, D. (2016). *The Biggest U.S. Tax Breaks*. Retrieved October 24, 2018, from Pew Research Center Website: http://www.pewresearch.org/fact-tank/2016/04/06/the-biggest-u-s-tax-breaks/

DeSilver, D. (2018, May 21). *U.S. Trails Most Developed Countries in Voter Turnout*. Retrieved June 28, 2019, from Pew Research Center Website: https://www.pewresearch.org/fact-tank/2018/05/21/u-s-voter-turnout-trails-most-developed-countries/

Foster, A., & Rojas, A. (2018). Program Participation and Spending Patterns of Families Receiving Government Means-Tested Assistance. *Monthly Labor Review*. https://doi.org/10.21916/mlr.2018.3.

Hamilton, L., & Martin-West, S. (2019). Universal Basic Income, Poverty, and Social Justice: A Moral and Economic Imperative for Social Workers. *Social Work, 64*(4), 321–328. https://doi.org/10.1093/sw/swz028.

Hamilton, L., & Mulvale, J. P. (2019). "Human Again": The (Unrealized) Promise of Basic Income in Ontario. *Journal of Poverty, 23*(7), 576–599. https://doi.org/10.1080/10875549.2019.1616242.

Johnson, J. D., Olivo, N., Gibson, N., Reed, W., & Ashburn-Nardo, L. (2009). Priming Media Stereotypes Reduces Support for Social Welfare Policies: The Mediating Role of Empathy. *Personality and Social Psychology Bulletin, 35*(4), 463–476. https://doi.org/10.1177/0146167208329856.

Li, H. (2017, August 24). *Which Areas Benefit Most From the Home Mortgage Interest Deduction?* Retrieved June 21, 2019, from Tax Foundation Website: https://taxfoundation.org/home-mortgage-interest-deduction-county-2017/

Limbert, W. M., & Bullock, H. E. (2005). 'Playing the Fool': US Welfare Policy from a Critical Race Perspective. *Feminism & Psychology, 15*(3), 253–274. https://doi.org/10.1177/0959-353505054715.

Linder, D. O. (1995). Juror Empathy and Race. *Tennessee Law Review, 63*, 887–916.

Misra, J. (2019, April 23). *Behind the 2018 U.S. Midterm Election Turnout.* Retrieved June 27, 2019, from The United States Census Bureau Website: https://www.census.gov/library/stories/2019/04/behind-2018-united-states-midterm-election-turnout.html

National Conference of State Legislatures. (2015). *Who We Elect: An Interactive Graphic.* Retrieved June 26, 2019, from http://www.ncsl.org/research/about-state-legislatures/who-we-elect-an-interactive-graphic.aspx

National Priorities Project. (2019). *Corporate Tax Breaks and the Federal Budget.* Retrieved from https://www.nationalpriorities.org/campaigns/corp-taxes-and-federal-budget/

Pew Research Center. (2019, May 1). *Historic Highs in 2018 Voter Turnout Extended Across Racial and Ethnic Groups.* Retrieved June 26, 2019, from Pew Research Center Website: https://www.pewresearch.org/fact-tank/2019/05/01/historic-highs-in-2018-voter-turnout-extended-across-racial-and-ethnic-groups/

Piven, F. F., & Cloward, R. (1993). *Regulating the Poor: The Functions of Public Welfare* (Updated, Subsequent ed.). New York: Vintage.

Rettig, J. (2010, July 8). Galston: Mandatory Voting Would Loosen Partisan Gridlock. *US News & World Report.* Retrieved from https://www.usnews.com/news/articles/2010/07/08/galston-mandatory-voting-would-loosen-partisan-gridlock

Schott, L., & Floyd, I. (2017). *How States Use Funds Under the TANF Block Grant.* Retrieved from Center for Budget Policies and Priorities Website: https://www.cbpp.org/research/family-income-support/how-states-use-funds-under-the-tanf-block-grant

Smith, C. (2018, May 9). *Why Economists Don't Like the Mortgage Interest Deduction.* Retrieved June 18, 2019, from Federal Reserve Bank of St. Louis Website: https://www.stlouisfed.org/open-vault/2018/may/why-economists-dont-like-mortgage-interest-deduction

Social Security Administration. (2019). *Social Security Administrative Expenses.* Retrieved June 19, 2019, from https://www.ssa.gov/OACT/STATS/admin.html

Standing, G. (2017). *Basic Income: A Guide for the Open-Minded.* New Haven, CT/London: Yale University Press.

Tax Policy Center. (2018). *How Are Capital Gains Taxed?* Retrieved from Urban Institute Website: https://www.taxpolicycenter.org/briefing-book/how-are-capital-gains-taxed

Thompson, D. (2017, May 14). The Shame of the Mortgage-Interest Deduction. *The Atlantic*. Retrieved from https://www.theatlantic.com/business/archive/2017/05/shame-mortgage-interest-deduction/526635/

Wilson, K. (2006). *Animal Strike at the Zoo. It's True*. New York: HarperCollins.

CHAPTER 7

The Most Vulnerable

Abstract The history of American child welfare policy includes a focus on removing children from poor parents, rather than supporting economically vulnerable families, a process which continues today. Increasingly stringent welfare eligibility criteria and the exclusion of millions of families from assistance has been directly linked with increased child poverty, child abuse, and foster care placements in the United States. The economic cost of growing childhood poverty, via increased crime, poorer health outcomes, and decreased economic productivity, is currently estimated at $1.03 trillion per year. Having no control over their parents' actions, children are the ultimate losers in the government's attempts to shape parental behavior. Conversely, improvements in child health, nutrition, well-being, and educational outcomes are a consistent finding of the various basic income experiments.

Keywords Children • Child welfare • Child poverty • Basic income

Regardless of one's position on the "worthiness" of low-income adults, most people agree that children deserve every possible support and opportunity. Unfortunately, the "crackdown" on welfare dependency in recent

---

Portions of this chapter appeared previously in Hamilton, L. (2011). *The foster parent bill of rights: An investigation of its perceived effectiveness in Arkansas.* University of Arkansas, Fayetteville, AR.

L. Hamilton, *Welfare Doesn't Work*, Exploring the Basic Income Guarantee, https://doi.org/10.1007/978-3-030-37121-0_7

decades has made children the ultimate losers in the government's attempts to shape parental behavior. The number of children living on less than $2 per day tripled between 1995 and 2012 (Shaefer & Edin, 2018). Of course, the Great Recession played a significant role in that increase, but the rate had already doubled by 2007, before the recession began. Researchers estimate that this pre-recession change is a direct result of Welfare Reform in 1996 (Shaefer & Edin, 2018).

The long-lasting effects of child poverty are well documented. Affected children have worse health outcomes, including lower birth weight, higher infant mortality, stunted physical development, and more hospitalizations than other children (Brooks-Gunn & Duncan, 1997). Growing up in poverty is also found to have a significant negative impact on brain development (McDermott et al., 2019). Children of low-income families have more developmental delays, learning disabilities, lower intelligence, poorer school performance, smaller vocabularies, and are more likely to drop out of high school. Low-income teen girls are more than three times as likely to become pregnant (Brooks-Gunn & Duncan, 1997). Research does not indicate that these are biologically inherited traits from low-income parents but rather result from lack of access to the health care, nutrition, and educational opportunities that middle- and upper-income families take for granted.

It is estimated that every dollar spent on preventing childhood poverty would save the economy at least $7 (Schoenherr, 2018). For example, while low-income children are nearly seven times as likely to be victims of abuse and neglect (Brooks-Gunn & Duncan, 1997), up to 30% of our current child protection expenditures could be prevented simply by ensuring that families have safe and stable housing (McLaughlin & Rank, 2018). The following discussion will explore the evolution of child welfare services in America, much of which has been necessary for the protection of children from abuse. However, we will also see that a great deal more effort is spent on protecting children from their parents, instead of supporting families, which creates better long-term outcomes for children and saves billions of dollars (Ringel et al., 2017).

A History of Child Welfare in America

Like many social policies, the history of child welfare in America first begins with the English Poor Laws. These laws were primarily concerned with ensuring that "poor" children did not inherit their parents' "sinful" ways. Not unlike today, the government assumed that the only explanation for poverty could be a character defect, rather than as a natural byproduct of an economic system that requires a perpetual underclass. In 1562, indentured servitude was formalized whereby orphaned child apprentices were placed with master artisans and their families (Whitelaw Downs, Moore, McFadden, & Costin, 2008). These placements were intended to provide (a) cheap labor for rapidly expanding industry, (b) a family environment for orphans, (c) the opportunity for low-income youth to learn a trade, and (d) an avenue for children of the poor to learn the "Christian" value of hard work. Apprenticeship became such a popular method for combating poverty that within 20 years, laws were established requiring all children (including non-orphans) to be placed in apprenticeships. If parents were unable to pay for such arrangements, parishes would coordinate placement, usually in lower-skilled trades (Leonard, 2013). This arrangement had the added benefits—to the government—of creating a mechanism of control over those in poverty and reducing public assistance costs.

Because many early American colonists were English Protestants, the Protestant work ethic played a significant role in early Colonial social policy (Karger & Stoesz, 2013). Protestants, believing that success on Earth signaled God's favor, valued production and self-sufficiency for both children and adults. Children were expected to contribute their labor to family farms from a very young age (Mallon & McCartt Hess, 2014). Those who came to America but who were abandoned or whose parents had died because of harsh living conditions in the colonies were often auctioned off to family farmers or apprenticed to tradespeople, usually by age eight or nine. As in England, children of very low-income families could be removed from their homes (Abramovitz, 1996). A 1646 Virginia law allowed children to be removed from poverty-stricken parents

> to be brought up in some good and lawful calling...for the better educating of youth in honest and profitable trades and manufactures... to avoid sloth and idleness wherewith such young children are easily corrupted... [and]... for the relief of such parents whose poverty extends not to give them good breeding. (Abramovitz, 1996, p. 70)

These practices gained public support out of a fear that orphans and the children of the poor might perpetuate the same "pauperism" that plagued England, so vividly described in the works of Charles Dickens. In 1824,

J.V.N. Yates, Secretary of State for New York, concluded a yearlong investigation of the numbers and living conditions of the impoverished. Yates advocated for an end to English-style indentured servitude and "outdoor relief." He perceived almshouses, or housing for the very poor of all ages, as a more humane alternative to bonded labor. He writes, "The education and morals of the children of paupers (except in almshouses) are almost wholly neglected" (Thurston, 1974, p. 24). Based on his recommendations and similar reports in other states, almshouses became a popular method of intervention for children living in poverty.

Later critics of Yates illuminated the potential harm of placing children with homeless, criminal, disabled, and mentally ill adults (Mallon & McCartt Hess, 2014). Almshouses were often overcrowded, provided wretched living conditions, and did little to protect children from abuse and exploitation by dangerous adults. Child advocates urged the increased use of orphanages, and most states passed laws banning the placement of children in almshouses by the late 1800s. According to the US Census Bureau, 10,718 children lived in American almshouses in 1880, but numbers declined to 2584 by 1923 (Thurston, 1974).

It is important to note, however, that this attention to child welfare was limited to the interests of *white* children, even though black family displacement was common in the slavery era and many children were without caregivers (Everett, Chipungu, & Leashore, 2004). Free black children were banned from private orphanages and remained mostly in state-funded almshouses or informal arrangements within the black community. Further, African American children were much more likely to be labeled as "delinquent" and sentenced to adult prisons. The first American orphanage for black children, known as the Philadelphia Association for the Care of Colored Children, was established in 1822 with private funds, but it was burned down by anti-abolitionists 16 years later (Mallon & McCartt Hess, 2014). Despite concerted efforts by the African American community to care for their orphaned children, early black orphanages were often "overcrowded and understaffed" (Everett et al., 2004, p. 3).

In the mid-1850s, immigration and poverty in America's eastern cities approached a crescendo. Millions of immigrants from Ireland, Germany, Poland and later, Eastern Europe, migrated to the US seeking employment in manufacturing and better living conditions. Escaping famine, almost 1.3 million Irish arrived in America between 1846 and 1855. Other immigrants, often Catholic or Jewish, sought relief from religious persecution and political instability in Europe (Cose, 1992). Industry proliferated so rapidly during this period that while four out of five Americans lived rurally in 1860, only two in five did in 1920 (Levine & Levine, 1992). As families moved from farms to urban environments in search of semi-skilled manufacturing jobs, they could no longer "live off the land" in lean times as they had before (Lederer & Jackson, 1990).

Rapid changes, including immigration, the transition from rural to urban living, and poor living conditions in city slums created new strains on family life. Adults and children, who had previously worked together on family farms, left home to spend long hours in dangerous and poorly paid industrial environments. Divorce rates increased dramatically, and many children lost one or both parents to factory accidents. As many as 30,000 children were homeless in New York City in any given year in the nineteenth century, and residents were anxious to address the growing number of young pickpockets and beggars (Levine & Levine, 1992).

Meanwhile, American leaders became increasingly concerned with maintaining cultural and political domination by Anglo-Saxon Protestants amid the rising tide Catholic and Jewish immigrants. Charles Loring Brace, a minister and social reformer of the mid-1800s, tapped into these intersecting fears by warning of roving bands of young, "unchurched" boys committing crime in America's eastern cities in his book, *The Dangerous Classes of New York*.

> Immigration is pouring in its multitude of poor foreigners, who leave these young outcasts everywhere abandoned in our midst. For the most part, the boys grow up utterly by themselves. No one cares for them, and they care for no one. Some live by begging, by petty pilfering, by bold robbery; some earn an honest support by peddling matches, or apples, or newspapers; others gather bones and rags in the street to sell. They sleep on steps, in cellars, in old barns, and in markets, or they hire a bed in filthy and low lodging-houses. They cannot read; they do not go to school or attend a church. Many of them have never seen the Bible. Every cunning faculty is intensely stimulated. They are shrewd and old in vice, when other children are in leading-strings. Few influences which are kind and good ever reach the vagrant boy. (Brace, 2010)

Without intervention, Brace envisioned societal breakdown and possible revolt by the children. He established the New York Children's Aid Society and the "child saving movement" by holding prayer meetings for homeless boys, with the hope of restoring order through religion (Levine & Levine,

1992). When this method proved ineffective, Brace recruited adoptive, farming families in upstate New York and the Midwest. He proposed "draining the city of these children," and launched the so-called Orphan Train Movement, which lasted through the early twentieth century (Brace, 2010).

Between 1854 and 1929, the movement removed more than 200,000 children from eastern cities and placed them with western farmers in the hopes—again—that they would adopt a (Protestant) Christian work ethic (Jansson, 2014). Controversy surrounded this movement. The Roman Catholic Church opposed the placements as many of the children descended from Catholic immigrants and were sent to live with Protestant adoptive families (Whittaker & Maluccio, 2002). Further, Brace's agents coerced impoverished families to relinquish their children and some agents may have "made money unscrupulously on the transactions" (Levine & Levine, 1992, p. 192). It was also later discovered that adoptive families were not thoroughly vetted and few follow-up visits were conducted. While many children were welcomed into loving homes, reports of child abuse and neglect were widespread (O'Connor, 2004).

These reports occurred at a time when the investigation of child abuse and neglect was in its infancy. A now-famous case among child welfare social workers is the plight of "Mary Ellen" in the 1870s, who was severely abused by her caretakers (Karger & Stoesz, 2013). Charity worker Etta Wheeler was unable to find help for Mary Ellen through local authorities since, at this time, children had few individual rights and were legally perceived as family "property" (Rodham, 1973). Wheeler turned to the New York Society for the Prevention of Cruelty to Animals to find a loophole through which she might gain protection for the young girl. With the help of the society, Mary Ellen was removed from her home three months after the initial discovery of the abuse. Her case spurred a public conversation about the rights of children and inspired the foundation of the New York Society for the Prevention of Cruelty to Children in 1874. Two hundred similar agencies existed across the country by 1900 (Mallon & McCartt Hess, 2014). The early focus of these societies was the prosecution of abuse, more than the provision of family support services, and as a result, the number of children removed from their parents increased. By 1900, most children in orphanages had at least one living parent (Abramovitz, 1996).

The turn of the century was a period of rapid change in American child welfare policy. Due to poor living conditions and through the work of child advocates, almshouses had largely fallen out of popularity and were replaced by orphanages and unpaid family homes. The ensuing years were dedicated to a debate regarding the relative merits and shortcomings of these two settings (Bremner, 1974). For example, the Catholic Church and Jewish communities both complained about the lack of appropriate family placements for non-protestant children. Indeed, many church denominations supported the continued use of orphanages, possibly related to the flow of state funds through religious institutions (Mallon & McCartt Hess, 2014).

The early twentieth century also witnessed a growth in the role of the federal government in child welfare. Until the First White House Conference on Children in 1909 and the establishment of the US Children's Bureau in 1912, states were largely left to determine child placement policy. Most states chose to fund private, religious orphanages and there was little, if any, focus upon keeping families together (Whittaker & Maluccio, 2002). Institutions were empowered to make reunification decisions and often maintained adversarial relationships with biological families. Most institutions provided religious instruction and job training for older children to ensure that they would become hard-working Christians as adults (Bremner, 1974). Agency workers were often wealthy volunteers and "had a vision of the patriarchal family and so were especially hard on single mothers" (Levine & Levine, 1992, p. 212). Children frequently stayed in out-of-home care long after they could have safely returned to their family (Mallon & McCartt Hess, 2014). Opponents of the federal Children's Bureau feared enhanced government oversight of the private sector and a restriction of states' rights. Notably, the private New York Society for the Prevention of Cruelty to Children, which oversaw the care of 15,000 children by 1890, fiercely fought the Children's Bureau Bill of 1912 (Bremner, 1974; Levine & Levine, 1992).

Again, it is important to note that black children remained largely peripheral in any organized child welfare system well into the early 1900s. Organizations such as the National Urban League advocated for the equitable treatment of orphaned black children, who were still cared for in informal arrangements within the black community, a few private orphanages, and "homes for working girls" (Billingsley, 1972; Mallon & McCartt Hess, 2014). Slowly, the increased use of extended family care in the early twentieth century created a place for black children in child welfare services as black families could be recruited and the politics of segregation avoided (Mallon & McCartt Hess, 2014).

Signs of Progress

Beginning with the Social Security Act of 1935, the mid-twentieth century saw several important advances in striking a balance between protecting children from abuse while supporting needy families to prevent harm in the first place. The establishment of Aid to Dependent Children (now TANF) shifted federal focus from temporary relief to the support of low-income families so that children might be maintained in their own homes. As a result, the number of children in out-of-home care began to sharply decrease (Bremner, 1974). Simultaneously, the Social Security Act created federal funds for child welfare services, formalizing child protective services in America for the first time. The act required states to create a plan for coordinated child welfare service delivery to qualify for block grants. By 1938, forty-nine states had submitted such plans (Mallon & McCartt Hess, 2014).

The mid-twentieth century also brought renewed attention to the plight of abused children. In 1962, Dr. Henry Kempe published a landmark paper, “The Battered Child Syndrome” (Rubin Williams, 1983). Aided by new advances in pediatric radiology, Dr. Kempe described young patients with injuries in multiple stages of healing, most likely the victims of long-term physical abuse. Doctors had previously been hesitant to accuse parents of abuse, preferring to respect familial privacy and the right of parents to discipline children. However, Dr. Kempe discovered that severely abused children were routinely overlooked by medical professionals and too frequently died from their injuries (Rubin Williams, 1983). This research stirred public outrage and contributed, in part, to the passage of the Child Abuse Prevention and Treatment Act of 1974 (CAPTA), which created federal funds to research, prevent, and treat child abuse (Rosenzweig, 2008). In addition, CAPTA created a national definition of child abuse and neglect and mandated the collection of child abuse statistics by states (Children’s Bureau, 2019).

The majority of children found to be abused or neglected in the 1970s were immediately funneled into the foster system (Raymond, 1999), with most children’s case files including a plan to remain in care until the age of 18 (Knitzer, 1981). Little emphasis existed on prevention or reunification services and, as a result, the number of children in foster care increased from approximately 8000 to 100,000 between 1970 and 1980 (Raymond, 1999). A disproportionately high number of the placed children were African American, with many ultimately adopted by white families, prompting advocacy groups such as the National Association of Black Social Workers to claim that the practice led to de facto cultural genocide (Editors, 1993).

Simultaneously, little oversight or data collection related to foster children and placements existed. In 1979, only 20 states required some form of external case review for children in foster care (Knitzer, 1981). A survey by the Children's Defense Fund in 1979 found that some agencies could not report the age of 49% of children in care or the legal status of 73% of foster children (Knitzer, 1981). As a result, foster children were often "lost" in the system, never to be in contact with or see their biological families again.

States had little fiscal incentive to improve. For example, before the passage of the Adoption Assistance and Child Welfare Act of 1980 (AACWA), federal child welfare funds were primarily allocated for foster care maintenance costs. The AFDC-Foster Care Program was established in 1961 and provided unlimited federal funds to match state foster care expenditures. By 1979, the program funneled roughly $200 million to state coffers (Knitzer, 1981). In essence, states were incentivized to place children in long-term foster care, as this allowed unlimited access to federal funds (Raymond, 1999).

Sponsors and advocates of AACWA sought to keep biological families intact and reduce the duration of time children spent in foster placement, simultaneously containing ballooning foster care costs (Samantrai, 1992). Passed in 1980, AACWA created a "carrot and stick" approach to reducing foster care "drift," a term used to describe children lingering in foster care and experiencing multiple placements. The act made federal foster care funds dependent upon states demonstrating "reasonable efforts" to prevent placement and to reunify families within eighteen months of foster placement (Raymond, 1999). The legislation also required that states provide prevention and reunification services to families. Finally, the act prompted the creation of database systems to track foster child data (e.g., demographic information, placement, and case plan statistics) (Knitzer, 1981).

Under AACWA, each child must have a written case plan reflecting that foster care placement is (a) located near the biological family's home, (b) able to accommodate any special needs, and (c) the "least restrictive environment" possible (i.e., children are not placed in residential treatment facilities if they can safely be cared for in a foster home) (Knitzer, 1981). Further, case plans are subject to administrative review every six months, and a judicial review must occur within 18 months of placement to make decisions regarding reunification, adoption, or long-term foster care. AACWA also opened legal proceedings to biological parents.

In a further attempt to address foster care drift, AACWA created adoption subsidies for "hard to place" children (minorities, sibling groups, or children with mental, emotional, or physical disabilities). It extended Medicaid to adopted children until the age of 18, as many adoptive parents were leery of children with foreseeably expensive medical care (Knitzer, 1981). These provisions made it possible for the adoption of thousands of children who might otherwise remain in foster care until adulthood.

A Hard Right Turn

Like all social policy, AACWA was not immune to the force of political tides. Enacted in the final months of President Carter's administration, AACWA was written to include sufficient funding and management for implementation. However, the newly elected Reagan administration froze all recent regulations in an effort to shrink federal bureaucracy. As a result, funding and oversight for AACWA diminished drastically. Reagan's administration proposed unsuccessful repeals of AACWA in 1981 and 1982. President Reagan was, however, successful in eliminating the performance-based funding provisions of AACWA and replaced them with block grants. Further, his focus on shrinking the federal bureaucracy removed the oversight mechanisms necessary to monitor compliance. Essentially, the "carrot and stick"–based policy ultimately contained neither (Samantrai, 1992).

Since the Reagan administration, appropriate implementation of AACWA has proven challenging. Research in the first two years after the bill's enactment found that some states implemented innovative prevention programs while others continued to prioritize intervention only after abuse and neglect occurred (Samantrai, 1992). Commentary in the ensuing 20 years involved the difficulty of enforcement, the vagueness of "reasonable efforts" language, and disagreement as to whether "reasonable efforts" should be required in situations where a child's life is in danger (Raymond, 1999). For example, to qualify for federal funds, youth courts must find that "reasonable efforts" were made to keep families intact.

> This administrative approach has rendered the reasonable efforts requirement useless-it now amounts to nothing more than a bureaucratic formality. The

> situation has become such a charade that many states now provide youth court orders that include boxes for the judges to check, to ensure that they do not forget to include the words 'reasonable efforts' in the order. (Raymond, 1999, p. 1254)

Without funding for oversight, it was nearly impossible to ensure nationwide implementation, which reflected AACWA's true legislative intent to prevent foster care placement and reunify families as quickly as possible.

In 1992, the US Supreme Court delivered a final blow to AACWA. In one of over 20 similar class-action suits (Suter v. Artist), the court found that the reasonable effort language was too vague and biological families, therefore, did not have "enforceable rights" (Kopels & Rycraft, 1993, p. 403). As a result, foster children and biological families have no legal redress if their case plans do not reach permanency within the required 18 months or if prevention services prove insufficient.

In 1997—one year after Welfare Reform and arguably as a result of the same Conservative swing in American politics—the Adoption and Safe Families Act (ASFA) was enacted, in part, to clear up confusion created by AACWA, but also subtly shifted focus from family preservation to adoption (Gelles, 1998). For example, AACWA placed priority on permanency planning and reasonable efforts toward reunification with the biological family. However, many practitioners were unclear as to the real meaning of "reasonable efforts." ASFA clarified that the health and safety of the child was paramount. Reasonable efforts toward reunification were not required if a biological parent had committed voluntary manslaughter, murder, or for a felony assault on their child (Gelles, 1998).

ASFA also shortened the timeline for completion of a permanency hearing. At the permanency hearing, judges make a final decision regarding whether the child will return to her parents, or proceed to adoption, legal guardianship, or another arrangement (Potter & Klein-Rothschild, 2002). Under AACWA, child welfare professionals had 18 months in which to determine a permanent plan for children; ASFA shortened this to 12 months. Finally, ASFA required the Termination of Parental Rights if a child has been in care for 15 of the past 22 months, is an abandoned infant, or if the parent has committed any of the crimes listed above (Gelles, 1998). Ultimately, this legislation shifted the focus of child welfare agencies to child safety (rather than family preservation), shortened the length of the average placement, and increased the number of annual adoptions (Mitchell et al., 2005).

The enactment of ASFA was met with both praise and criticism. State child welfare workers felt that it did not give parents enough time to complete treatment plans (Gelles, 1998). For example, among parents struggling with addiction (representing as much as a third of foster care cases) (Sepulveda & Williams, 2019), it can be challenging to reach sustainable sobriety within 12 months. It is also more difficult to find long-term placements for some children, including those who are older, African American, or have disabilities (Potter & Klein-Rothschild, 2002). Judges are allowed to make exceptions in such cases, and as a result, many children remain in foster care longer than the maximum 12 months (Raphel, 2008).

Child development experts understand that instability in the early years has significant consequences, and therefore, establishing permanency quickly ultimately benefits children. However, taken in context of declining support to families in need as described in earlier chapters, one can argue that the colonial policy of removing children from poor parents—in essence blaming those in poverty rather than addressing the larger economic factors at play—has only marginally improved since the country's founding.

Welfare Outcomes for Children

Child welfare reform efforts that give families less time to complete treatment plans and incentivize states to prioritize adoptions, combined with increasing TANF restrictions, have created the perfect storm for financially vulnerable families. Between 1985 and 2000, the number of children in foster care more than doubled from 276,000 to a historic high of 578,000 (Swann & Sylvester, 2006). This outcome is especially surprising given the passage of the Adoption and Safe Families of 1997 which emphasized faster permanency. Two researchers examined several possible explanations for the increase, including state poverty and unemployment rates, violent crime rates, state political makeup, the number of working mothers or "absent" fathers, TANF caseloads, and the female incarceration rate. The latter two criteria were the strongest predictors of foster care caseloads. The authors hypothesized that the War on Drugs and Welfare Reform had significantly increased the number of children in foster care (Swann & Sylvester, 2006).

More recent data suggest that the situation has improved slightly from peak highs around the turn of the millennium. On an average day in 2017, there were 442,995 children in American foster homes (Children's Bureau, 2017). Of course, the total population of the United States has changed since the 1980s, making raw data difficult to interpret. In 1990, the total proportion of children in care was 6.2 foster children for every 1000 American children, compared to six out of every 1000 in 2017, with a historic peak of 7.9 in 1999 (Child Trends Databank, 2019). Recent reductions may be partly explained by a decrease in the number of children in foster care for more than five years, declining from 10% of all foster children in 1999 to 4% in 2017 (Child Trends Databank, 2019). Of children leaving foster care in 2017, the average length of stay was 19.2 months, down from 21.7 months in 2003 (Children's Bureau, 2006, 2018). This is a positive change for children, as permanency is critical to child development. However, increasingly, foster children are adopted rather than returned to their biological parents. In 2003, 18% of children who exited foster care were adopted, compared to 24% in 2017 (Children's Bureau, 2006, 2018).

While the child welfare system has created faster permanency for children in foster care, we must ask why fewer children are remaining with or returning to their biological families. Harsh welfare eligibility criteria and declining caseloads appear to play an important role. Losing TANF benefits after a child is placed in foster care decreases the likelihood that the family will be reunified (Kortenkamp, Geen, & Stagner, 2004). Among TANF households, sanctions for non-compliance is linked with increased child abuse and poorer school performance (Larson, Singh, & Lewis, 2011; Slack, Lee, & Berger, 2007). In other words, removing support from financially vulnerable families increases stress, makes effective parenting more challenging, and puts children at risk for foster care placement and adoption. Rather than support economically vulnerable households, we are increasingly moving to terminate parental rights and place children for adoption.

This policy choice carries significant costs for American taxpayers. While the TANF budget in 2017 was roughly double that for all foster care services ($16.73 billion versus $8.06 billion) (Administration for Children and Families, 2016), TANF serves nearly four times as many children. An average of 1.76 million children receive TANF (not to mention their 491,216 parents and caregivers), compared to the average of 442,995 children in foster care (Administration for Children and Families, 2018;

Children's Bureau, 2017). This variation is partially due to significant differences in administrative costs. Families involved with child welfare services require monthly meetings with a caseworker—at a minimum—and considerable court involvement. In my experience, each child welfare case involved one caseworker for the family, another for the foster family, separate attorneys to represent the family and the government agency, often a Guardian ad Litem to represent the interests of the child (although this a volunteer position in some states), and administrative structures to supervise all of these workers. Further, even when children are adopted from foster care, 93% continue to receive monthly subsidies until the child turns 18 (Children's Bureau, 2018).

Eliminating poverty would not prevent 100% of child abuse, and we will always need structures to protect vulnerable children. However, we can also see that child protective services have historically de-emphasized the support and maintenance of economically marginalized families. Instead, children are removed from families only after the situation has become dangerous. The long-term consequences of this practice are devastating both to children and society at large. While limited, basic income research suggests that child outcomes will drastically improve by providing a functional safety net to all families.

Basic Income Outcomes for Children

A consistent finding of the various basic income experiments is improvements in childhood outcomes. Multiple pilots discovered improved test scores, better school attendance, and lower high school dropout rates (Marinescu, 2017; Salkind & Haskins, 1982). Some research has found that basic income makes children as much as 90% more likely to complete high school (Maynard & Murnane, 1979). The most significant gains appear among children who had previously been living in poverty and who were comparatively younger when their family began receiving a basic income (Marinescu, 2017). In the Manitoba experiment of the 1970s, community-wide high school dropout rates were lower than in similar areas without a basic income (Forget, 2011).

Research also suggests that child recipients are healthier and have better nutrition as a result of basic income. Women receiving basic income have fewer children and get more prenatal care (Marinescu, 2017; Ruckert, Huynh, & Labonté, 2017). In both the Gary, Indiana experiment and Alaska Permanent Fund, infant birth weights increased (Marinescu, 2017).

Here too, the greatest gains appeared among low-income families. Global basic-income pilots in Namibia and India both discovered improvements in child nutrition and school attendance (Davala, Jhabvala, Standing, & Mehta, 2015; Haarmann et al., 2008).

One longitudinal study of 1420 children across 11 counties in Western North Carolina beginning in 1993 provided an accidental, in-depth look at the effects of basic income (Akee, Simeonova, Costello, & Copeland, 2015). The Eastern Band of Cherokees is based in this region and roughly a quarter of the children in the study were Native American. In 1997, the tribe opened a casino and began distributing dividends to every adult member of the tribe, averaging $4000 per person annually (Marinescu, 2017). Because of the benefit, between 1993 and 2000, the percentage of Native American households in the study with incomes higher than $30,000 per year climbed from 20% to 60%. The researchers compared Native children in households that began receiving dividends when the children were 9–11 years old with those who were older. A comparison was also made between the younger Native children and white children not receiving dividends. Native children who began receiving dividends at a young age had comparatively better mental health outcomes, better parent–child relationships, were less likely to use or deal drugs, less likely to be arrested, and more likely to graduate high school (Akee et al., 2015; Yoshikawa, Aber, & Beardslee, 2012).

Interviews with recipients in other UBI pilots help to explain these improvements. One Ontario participant described how the boost to household finances improved her mental health and resultantly, her parenting.

> I took two months to get my anxiety under control [after joining the pilot]. I found a full-time job in a little less than two months…my kids confidence went higher. [They] started bringing home better grades.…They have proper winter clothing … [are] able to play outside.…Basic income made me want to better myself and I did.…Nothing but positive in this household. Thank you, basic income. (Basic Income Canada Network, 2019)

Another mother explained that "this pilot has given me the chance to spend more time with my children.…A stable house and a stable mom not worrying about putting food on the table or gas in my vehicle to go to work" (Basic Income Canada Network, 2019).

A basic income to all adults is not the only avenue for improving the lives of children. Many European countries and Canada offer a universal child allowance. These benefits range from US$2400 annually for two children in the Netherlands to US$56,000 in Belgium and Germany (Shaefer et al., 2018). Like a basic income, these credits are unconditional. Because we lack child allowances, after accounting for all types of income and tax-transfer programs (including SNAP, TANF, housing assistance, the EITC, and similar programs in the United States), America has one of the highest childhood poverty rates among OECD countries, surpassed only by Bulgaria, Romania, Greece, Mexico, Israel, and Turkey (Shaefer et al., 2018).

However it is ultimately implemented, financial investments in children, especially young and low-income children, have remarkable effects on their long term health, educational outcomes, and their economic productivity in adulthood. Based on the number of student essays, I read beginning with the phrase "Children are the future," this point seems to be relatively uncontroversial in the United States. What we tend to de-emphasize is precisely *how* these improvements come about. Put simply, children's lives improve when their parent's lives improve. When parents have income stability and less economic stress, they become better parents and spend more quality time with their children. They also have the resources to access medical care, better schools, quality childcare, and the kind of enrichment opportunities more common to middle- and upper-income children.

While hackneyed, I often remind my students that if you want a plant to grow, you pour water on the soil below it, not on the leaves. Until we decide to stop punishing low-income parents for economic circumstances outside of their control, children will continue to pay the price. And so will the economy. If estimates are correct that $1 spent on preventing childhood poverty reaps $7 in economic savings (Schoenherr, 2018), a universal basic income quickly pays for itself.

References

Abramovitz, M. (1996). *Regulating the Lives of Women: Social Welfare Policy from Colonial Times to the Present.* Boston: South End Press.

Administration for Children and Families. (2016, February 16). *FY 2017 Budget in Brief.* Retrieved from HHS.gov Website: https://www.hhs.gov/about/budget/fy2017/budget-in-brief/acf/mandatory/index.html

Administration for Children and Families. (2018). *TANF Caseload Data 2018*. Retrieved from Office of Family Assistance Website: https://www.acf.hhs.gov/ofa/resource/tanf-caseload-data-2018

Akee, R., Simeonova, E., Costello, E. J., & Copeland, W. (2015). *How Does Household Income Affect Child Personality Traits and Behaviors?* (Working Paper No. 21562). https://doi.org/10.3386/w21562.

Basic Income Canada Network. (2019). *Signposts to Success: Report of a BICN Survey of Ontario Basic Income Recipients*. Retrieved from Basic Income Canada Network Website: https://www.basicincomecanada.org/time_for_national_action_new_report_shows_ontario_basic_income_pilot_was_on_track_to_success?fbclid=IwAR1BcwCr6pQ-kLHv_YRXddbK48jv2OLH9pGX-X1rU_946RB-Kvro2wvVrCg

Billingsley, A. (1972). *Children of the Storm: Black Children and American Child Welfare*. New York: Harcourt College Pub.

Brace, C. L. (2010). *The Dangerous Classes of New York, and Twenty Years' Work Among Them*. Retrieved from https://www.gutenberg.org/ebooks/33431

Bremner, R. H. (1974). *Children and Youth in America: A Documentary History*. Boston: Harvard University Press.

Brooks-Gunn, J., & Duncan, G. J. (1997). The Effects of Poverty on Children. *The Future of Children, 7*(2), 55–71. https://doi.org/10.2307/1602387.

Child Trends Databank. (2019). *Foster Care*. Retrieved from Child Trends Website: https://www.childtrends.org/indicators/foster-care

Children's Bureau. (2006). *The AFCARS Report Interim FY 2003 Estimates as of June 2006*. Retrieved from https://www.acf.hhs.gov/sites/default/files/cb/afcarsreport10.pdf

Children's Bureau. (2017). *Foster Care Statistics 2017*. Retrieved from Child Welfare Information Gateway Website: https://www.childwelfare.gov/pubPDFs/foster.pdf

Children's Bureau. (2018). *The AFCARS Report: Preliminary FY 2017 Estimates* (No. 25). Retrieved from https://www.acf.hhs.gov/sites/default/files/cb/afcarsreport25.pdf

Children's Bureau. (2019). *About CAPTA: A Legislative History* (p. 3). Retrieved from Administration for Children and Families Website: https://www.childwelfare.gov/pubPDFs/about.pdf

Cose, E. (1992). *A Nation of Strangers: Prejudice, Politics, and the Populating of America* (1st ed.). New York: William Morrow & Co.

Davala, S., Jhabvala, R., Standing, G., & Mehta, S. K. (2015). *Basic Income: A Transformative Policy for India*. London/New Delhi, India: Bloomsbury Academic.

Editors. (1993, November 27). Black Children, White Parents. *The New York Times*. Retrieved from https://www.nytimes.com/1993/11/27/opinion/black-children-white-parents.html

Everett, J. E., Chipungu, S. S., & Leashore, B. R. (Eds.). (2004). *Child Welfare Revisited: An Africentric Perspective* (2nd ed.). New Brunswick, NJ: Rutgers University Press.

Forget, E. L. (2011). The Town with No Poverty: The Health Effects of a Canadian Guaranteed Annual Income Field Experiment. *Canadian Public Policy, 37*(3), 283–305. https://doi.org/10.3138/cpp.37.3.283.

Gelles, R. J. (1998). The Adoption and Safe Families Act of 1997 Rightly Places Child Safety First. *Brown University Child & Adolescent Behavior Letter, 14*(4), 1.

Haarmann, C., Haarmann, D., Jauch, H., Shindonola-Mote, H., Nattrass, N., Samson, M., & Standing, G. (2008). *Towards a Basic Income Grant for All: Basic Income Grant Pilot Project Assessment Report, September 2008*. Retrieved from NANGOF Website: http://www.bignam.org/Publications/BIG_Assessment_report_08a.pdf

Hill, M. S., & Sandfort, J. R. (1995). Effects of Childhood Poverty on Productivity Later in Life: Implications for Public Policy. *Children and Youth Services Review, 17*(1), 91–126. https://doi.org/10.1016/0190-7409(95)00005-W.

Jansson, B. S. (2014). *The Reluctant Welfare State: Engaging History to Advance Social Work Practice in Contemporary Society* (8th ed.). Belmont, CA: Cengage Learning.

Karger, H. J., & Stoesz, D. (2013). *American Social Welfare Policy: A Pluralist Approach* (7th ed.). Boston: Pearson.

Knitzer, J. (1981). Child Welfare: The Role of Federal Policies. *Journal of Clinical Child Psychology, 10*(1), 3–7. https://doi.org/10.1080/15374418109533003.

Kopels, S., & Rycraft, J. R. (1993). The U.S. Supreme Court Rules on Reasonable Efforts: A Blow to Child Advocacy. *Child Welfare, 72*(4), 397–406.

Kortenkamp, K., Geen, R., & Stagner, M. (2004). The Role of Welfare and Work in Predicting Foster Care Reunification Rates for Children of Welfare Recipients. *Children and Youth Services Review, 26*(6), 577–590. https://doi.org/10.1016/j.childyouth.2004.02.012.

Larson, A. M., Singh, S., & Lewis, C. (2011). Sanctions and Education Outcomes for Children in TANF Families. *Child & Youth Services, 32*(3), 180–199.

Lederer, W. J., & Jackson, D. D. (1990). *The Mirages of Marriage* (Reprint ed.). New York: W. W. Norton & Company.

Leonard, E. M. (2013). *The Early History of English Poor Relief* (1st ed.). Cambridge, UK: Cambridge University Press.

Levine, M., & Levine, A. (1992). *Helping Children: A Social History* (Subsequent ed.). New York: Oxford University Press.

Mallon, G., & McCartt Hess, P. (Eds.). (2014). *Child Welfare for the Twenty-first Century: A Handbook of Practices, Policies, and Programs* (2nd ed.). New York: Columbia University Press.

Marinescu, I. (2017). *No Strings Attached: The Behavioral Effects of U.S. Unconditional Cash Transfer Programs*. Retrieved from Roosevelt Institute

Website: http://rooseveltinstitute.org/wp-content/uploads/2017/05/No-Strings-Attached-050417-1.pdf

Maynard, R. A., & Murnane, R. J. (1979). The Effects of a Negative Income Tax on School Performance: Results of an Experiment. *The Journal of Human Resources, 14*(4), 463–476. https://doi.org/10.2307/145317.

McDermott, C. L., Seidlitz, J., Nadig, A., Liu, S., Clasen, L. S., Blumenthal, J. D., et al. (2019). Longitudinally Mapping Childhood Socioeconomic Status Associations with Cortical and Subcortical Morphology. *Journal of Neuroscience, 39*(8), 1365–1373. https://doi.org/10.1523/JNEUROSCI.1808-18.2018.

McLaughlin, M., & Rank, M. R. (2018). Estimating the Economic Cost of Childhood Poverty in the United States. *Social Work Research, 42*(2), 73–83. https://doi.org/10.1093/swr/svy007.

Mitchell, L., Barth, R., Green, R., Wall, A., Biemer, P., Berrick, J., & Webb, M. (2005). Child Welfare Reform in the United States: Findings from a Local Agency Survey. *Child Welfare, 84*(1), 5–24.

O'Connor, S. (2004). *Orphan Trains: The Story of Charles Loring Brace and the Children He Saved and Failed* (1st ed.). Chicago: University of Chicago Press.

Potter, C., & Klein-Rothschild, S. (2002). Getting Home on Time: Predicting Timely Permanence for Young Children. *Child Welfare, 81*(2), 123–150.

Raphel, S. (2008). Eye on Washington. Kinship Care and the Situation for Grandparents. *Journal of Child & Adolescent Psychiatric Nursing, 21*(2), 118–120.

Raymond, S. L. (1999). Where Are the Reasonable Efforts to Enforce the Reasonable Efforts Requirement?: Monitoring State Compliance Under the Adoption Assistance and Child Welfare Act of 1980. *Texas Law Review, 77*(5), 1235.

Ringel, J. S., Schultz, D., Mendelsohn, J., Holliday, S. B., Sieck, K., Edochie, I., & Davis, L. (2017). *Improving Children's Lives.* Retrieved from Rand Corporation Website: https://www.rand.org/pubs/research_briefs/RB9949-1.html

Rodham, H. (1973). Children Under the Law. *Harvard Educational Review, 43*(4), 487–514. https://doi.org/10.17763/haer.43.4.e14676283875773k.

Rosenzweig, J. (2008). Child Abuse and Neglect: Public Systems and Private Lives. *Kennedy School Review, 8*, 115–116.

Rubin Williams, G. J. (1983). Editorial: Child Protection: A Journey into History. *Journal of Clinical Child Psychology, 12*(3), 236–243. https://doi.org/10.1080/15374418309533138.

Ruckert, A., Huynh, C., & Labonté, R. (2017). Reducing Health Inequities: Is Universal Basic Income the Way Forward? *Journal of Public Health, 40*, 1–5. https://doi.org/10.1093/pubmed/fdx006.

Salkind, N., & Haskins, R. (1982). Negative Income Tax: The Impact on Children from Low-Income Families. *Journal of Family Issues, 3*(2), 165–180. https://doi.org/10.1177/019251382003002003.

Samantrai, K. (1992). To Prevent Unnecessary Separation of Children and Families: Public Law 96–272—Policy and Practice. *Social Work, 37*(4), 295–302. https://doi.org/10.1093/sw/37.4.295.
Schoenherr, N. (2018, April 16). *Childhood Poverty Costs U.S. $1.03 Trillion in a Year, Study Finds.* Retrieved October 24, 2018, from The Source Website: https://source.wustl.edu/2018/04/childhood-poverty-cost-u-s-1-03-trillion-in-a-year-study-finds/
Sepulveda, K., & Williams, S. C. (2019, February 25). *One in Three Children Entered Foster Care in 2017 Because of Parental Drug Abuse.* Retrieved from Child Trends Website: https://www.childtrends.org/one-in-three-children-entered-foster-care-in-fy-2017-because-of-parental-drug-abuse
Shaefer, H. L., Collyer, S., Duncan, G., Edin, K., Garfinkel, I., Harris, D., et al. (2018). A Universal Child Allowance: A Plan to Reduce Poverty and Income Instability Among Children in the United States. *RSF: The Russell Sage Foundation Journal of the Social Sciences, 4*(2), 22–42.
Shaefer, H. L., & Edin, K. (2018). *Welfare Reform and the Families It Left Behind* (pp. 22–27). Retrieved from Stanford Center on Poverty & Inequality Website: https://inequality.stanford.edu/sites/default/files/Pathways_Winter2018_Families-Left-Behind.pdf
Slack, K. S., Lee, B. J., & Berger, L. M. (2007). Do Welfare Sanctions Increase Child Protection System Involvement? A Cautious Answer. *Social Service Review, 81*(2), 207–228.
Swann, C. A., & Sylvester, M. S. (2006). The Foster Care Crisis: What Caused Caseloads to Grow? *Demography, 43*(2), 309–335.
Thurston, H. W. (1974). *The Dependent Child.* New York: Arno Press.
Whitelaw Downs, S., Moore, E., McFadden, E. J., & Costin, L. B. (2008). *Child Welfare and Family Services: Policies and Practice* (8th ed.). Boston: Pearson Education.
Whittaker, J. K., & Maluccio, A. N. (2002). Rethinking "Child Placement": A Reflective Essay. *Social Service Review, 76*(1), 108–134. https://doi.org/10.1086/324610.
Yoshikawa, H., Aber, L., & Beardslee, W. (2012). The Effects of Poverty on the Mental, Emotional, and Behavioral Health of Children and Youth: implications for Prevention. *American Psychologist, 67*(4), 272–284.

CHAPTER 8

The Alternative

Abstract Unconditional cash transfers are not entirely foreign in the United States. Now eclipsing TANF as the primary poverty alleviation program, the Earned Income Tax Credit (EITC) is associated with improved health and educational outcomes and does not carry employment disincentives. However, UBI carries several advantages to the EITC including greater bargaining power for workers and supporting unpaid care work. While there are many ways to implement UBI, tax-based proposals, such as the Negative Income Tax, may be most appealing to a skeptical American public. Those interested in eradicating poverty, dismantling a social safety net that primarily serves to punish the poor, and removing barriers to long-term financial stability are encouraged to contact their representatives in Congress and join basic income advocacy groups.

Keywords Earned Income Tax Credit • Basic income • Negative Income Tax

The idea of unconditional cash transfers is not entirely foreign in the United States. The Earned Income Tax Credit (EITC is a refundable credit for low- and moderate-income households and has now eclipsed TANF as the primary anti-poverty program in the United States, comprising $77 billion of the annual federal budget and lifting 8.9 million

L. Hamilton, *Welfare Doesn't Work*, Exploring the Basic Income Guarantee, https://doi.org/10.1007/978-3-030-37121-0_8

Americans out of poverty in 2016 (Center on Budget and Policy Priorities, 2018c; DeSilver, 2016). Similar to basic income, the EITC is associated with improved health and educational outcomes and does not carry the same employment disincentives as income-restricted programs like TANF, SNAP, and SSI (Marr, Huang, Sherman, & Debot, 2015).

While many prefer to support programs that funnel money past parents and directly to children, EITC has a more positive effect on child educational outcomes than even the Head Start preschool program (Whitehurst, 2001). Public Pre-K, while valuable, has produced mixed educational results, with some research suggesting that any developmental benefits are lost by early elementary school (Piper, 2019). Some experts hypothesize that gains seen in Head Start are not necessarily dependent on the curriculum content, but on the fact that the program provides essential childcare, allowing low-income parents to work or go to school, and better support their families (Piper, 2018).

Because the EITC encourages work, expands the tax base, and reduces the need for other family support programs, like many basic income trials, the net cost to taxpayers is roughly 13 cents per dollar dispersed ("The Earned Income Tax Credit almost pays for itself," 2018). However, some economists argue that a basic income is still preferable to the EITC, which carries several critical flaws. First, because the demand for labor is finite, the EITC encourages some people to work more but ultimately reduces job availability for others. Second, the EITC has been found to suppress wages because it allows employers to pay less than a living wage, with the tax credit filling in the gaps for working families. If instead, workers had a UBI, they would have stronger bargaining power to demand living wages from their employers. Further, tax credits like the EITC do little to support those (predominantly women) who contribute millions in unpaid care work to the economy. Finally, non-universal programs like the EITC and other poverty alleviation efforts are always more politically precarious than universal programs that benefit all citizens, like Social Security (Kasy, 2018).

Unconditional cash transfers are also significantly more efficient than in-kind (food, housing vouchers, etc.) or conditional programs because they remove significant layers of bureaucracy. For example, the World Food Program, which has historically distributed food to people in developing countries, has begun switching to direct cash aid as it has found that this creates better nutritional outcomes for less money (Hoddinott et al., n.d.).

How Would a Basic Income Work?

There are multiple proposals for exactly how to implement a basic income and many other books outline the possibilities in detail. Here, I will only attempt to describe a few potential approaches. First, some advocates propose to transform the EITC and the majority of means-tested poverty programs into a Negative Income Tax (NIT), which is a refundable tax credit bringing every household to the federal poverty level and phasing out slowly as income increases. Some calculations find that offering basic income even to high-income households comes with a hefty price tag and would either increase our national deficit or increase the marginal tax rate, both of which might be political non-starters (Nikiforos, Steinbaum, & Zezza, 2017; Widerquist, 2017). Conversely, an NIT is potentially cheaper than our current poverty alleviation efforts (Wiederspan, Rhodes, & Shaefer, 2015). The most effective way to do this is to decrease the credit slowly (e.g., a $0.50 reduction for each $1.00 increase in earned income) so that there is never a penalty for work.

Researchers at the University of Michigan calculated what this might look like in practice. If a family had no income, their tax credit would be 100% of the poverty line ($20,780 for a family of three) (US Department of Health and Human Services, 2019). If the family's earned income increased to half the poverty line ($10,390), their tax credit would decrease to $15,585. The credit would phase out completely once the family's income reached twice the poverty level ($41,560). This plan would cost roughly $219 billion per year and could be almost completely paid for by replacing most or all of our current poverty programs (Wiederspan et al., 2015).

Alternatively, Karl Widerquist, a prominent UBI advocate, recommends a $12,000 annual benefit to each adult and $6000 to each child combined with a flat 50% marginal tax rate (Widerquist, 2017). Households with incomes less than $5000, $5000–$9999, and $10,000–$14,999 would gain a mean net household income of $20,729, $22,711, and $24,050, respectively. The UBI would eventually phase out at the $55,000 household income level since additional earned income is taxed at 50%. Assuming a 0.7% administrative cost (borrowed from the relatively simple to administer Social Security program), and without replacing any existing social programs or tax expenditures, the total net cost to American taxpayers would be $539 billion per year. Of course, a 50% flat tax rate may be politically contentious. For this reason, Widerquist reruns his analysis by dropping the tax rate for households above the "break-even" point to 25%. In this calculation, the net cost is $654 billion.

Any new major social policy, including both the Social Security Act of 1935 and Medicare/Medicaid in 1965, is attacked on the grounds that it will not work or would have unintended negative consequences. While opponents argue that either increasing taxes or the national deficit to finance a UBI scheme would be disastrous, economists at the Levy Institute calculated the economic effects of various financing schemes (Nikiforos et al., 2017). Interestingly, they find that if we were to pay for a UBI through increased taxes, the American economy would grow slightly since people with low incomes are more likely to spend additional income than upper-income households (because they have more unmet spending needs), with positive downstream effects on wages and employment. But this research also finds that giving every American adult $1000 per month, entirely financed by increasing the national debt, would grow the economy by 12.56% *beyond* typical growth forecasts within eight years. It is common for people to be uncomfortable with the idea of increasing national debt. However, in some circumstances, it is warranted. For example, at the household level, if one could hypothetically borrow money at an annual 2% interest rate and then reinvest that money into a savings account that yields 5%, borrowing money is actually the sound financial decision.

Other proposals include taking a basic income entirely outside of government control. For example, some advocates see a path for financing UBI through the growing cryptocurrency market (Rice, 2019). Another proposal, by Robert Stanton, involves the creation of solar power co-ops, which generate income for every citizen (Stayton, 2019). In this scenario, anyone on Earth can sign up to be the owner of a ten-kW solar panel for free (maintained by solar farms), to be paid back with the first few years of dividends. Because businesses and manufacturers consume roughly two-thirds of all power, they would finance the majority of dividends to co-op members. Stanton estimates that the majority of the planet's power needs could be provided with solar panels roughly equivalent to the size of Texas, although they would be strategically placed throughout the world. This ambitious proposal seeks to simultaneously address the two most pressing issues of our time: growing inequality and climate change.

Of course, the primary hurdle to implementing any basic income scheme is a political one. It is promising though that the current basic income coalition includes the diverse support of Silicon Valley tech entrepreneurs, academics, social justice advocates, Libertarians, and economists. There have also been a few basic-income-like proposals in Congress. For example, in 2019, Senator Kamala Harris introduced the LIFT the Middle Class Act, a refundable tax credit giving up to $6000 per year to low-income working families (Wright, 2018). However, basic income activists expressed concern that these types of work credit proposals leave out those who are not in the workforce. A few months later, Representative Rashida Tlaib expanded on the proposal, introducing a similar credit, but including those with no income (Stein, 2019).

Tax-based proposals may be the best way to introduce basic income to a skeptical American public and simultaneously simplify an unnecessarily complex tax code if it were to absorb some of the less effective credits discussed in earlier chapters. In Table 8.1, we see that absorbing the major poverty programs and tax credits in the United States quickly pays for either an NIT or Widerquist's more generous proposal described earlier.

More moderate ideas include Senator Cory Booker's "baby bonds" bill, which would place $1000 in a savings account, controlled by the Treasury Department, for every child born in America. The program would then make annual additions to the accounts, based on parental

Table 8.1 Potential funding sources for basic income in the United States

Program	*Annual cost in billions*
SSI[a]	59
TANF[b]	16.5
SNAP[c]	70
Lower tax rates on dividends and capital gains[d]	134.6
Mortgage interest deduction[e]	77
Deductions of state and local taxes[f]	65.1
Refundable tax credits (including EITC)[g]	213
Total	**635.2**

Source: Author's creation

[a]Center on Budget and Policy Priorities (2018b)

[b]Floyd, Pavetti, and Schott (2015)

[c]Center on Budget and Policy Priorities (2018d)

[d]DeSilver (2016)

[e]Ibid.

[f]Ibid.

[g]Congressional Budget Office (2013)

income, of up to $2000 for children in the lowest-income families. When a child turns 18, they could use these funds to pursue an education, buy a home, or start a business (Corasaniti, 2019). While ambitious, basic-income advocates worry that this bill still diverts funding around parents who are the most important predictors of child outcomes, and inserts paternalistic rules into exactly how the money is spent.

Finally, the 2020 Democratic Presidential Primary candidate Andrew Yang ran on a platform primarily focused on basic income. A former tech entrepreneur, Yang proposed to provide $1000 per month to every American adult (Rodrigo, 2019). While Yang's campaign was a long shot, the fact that he was running in a major party primary and garnered even 2% of the vote in a Quinnipiac University Poll suggests that the idea is gaining some degree of mainstream attention (Quinnipiac University, 2019).

Would the Poor Be Worse Off?

Before any such proposal is adopted, we must ensure that vulnerable families will not be left with even fewer resources. Unfortunately, determining the real value of current programs is difficult and highly political. For example, the Census Bureau's Survey of Income and Program Participation calculates the average combined monthly benefit across four major assistance programs at $404 per person (Irving & Loveless, 2015). However, this estimate leaves out many essential "in-kind" (i.e., noncash) benefits. Attempting to address this gap, the conservative Cato Institute calculated the total benefit to a family of four who was hypothetically receiving aid from TANF, SNAP, housing vouchers, Women, Infants and Children (for pregnant women and their children up to age five), the Low Income Home Energy Assistance Program, the Emergency Food Assistance Program (a food bank distribution program), and Medicaid (Tanner & Hughes, 2013). For our purposes, I will subtract the value of Medicaid, since few basic income proposals advocate for its replacement.

The remaining programs, according to Cato, would provide an average annual value (in cash and in-kind benefits) of $20,492. This amount is significantly less than NIT proposals, which would provide a family of four with $25,100 (if the family had no other income) or Widerquist's basic-income proposal at $36,000 (assuming the family includes two adults and two children) (Widerquist, 2017; Wiederspan et al., 2015). Only 11 states (HI, DC, MA, CT, NJ, RI, NY, VT, NH, MD, and CA), hypothetically provide an annual benefit above $25,100. The difference in these states is due to higher real estate values and necessarily higher housing vouchers, suggesting that some states may need to continue providing housing assistance to supplement basic income. Some proposals also recommend absorption of the EITC, but this program offers an average annual benefit of $3176, still bringing the total value below most NIT and basic-income proposals (Center on Budget and Policy Priorities, 2018c; Wiederspan et al., 2015).

While these figures should give UBI advocates pause, the Cato Institute report contains several serious weaknesses. For example, it estimates a hypothetical monthly SNAP benefit of $517, when the average is actually $249 (Center on Budget and Policy Priorities, 2018a). But it is useful because, for political reasons, it's the most generous possible calculation of our current social safety net. Politicians have already cited it to argue that generous welfare programs pay more than many full-time jobs and therefore remove work incentives (Yee Hee Lee, 2014a). Ironically, these claims usually lead to even greater restrictions on eligibility that only *further* disincentivize work and trap families in poverty.

The primary flaw in the Cato Institute's estimate is that very few households receive assistance from all of these programs at once. The Urban Institute analyzed the services low-income families (up to 200% of the poverty line) *actually* receive and included the same programs as mentioned earlier, plus Supplemental Security Income (for citizens with disabilities), the school lunch program, and vouchers for transportation or childcare (Edelstein, Pergamit, & Ratcliffe, 2014). In practice, 57% of low-income families receive assistance from one, two, or three programs, 20% receive support from more than three, and 22% receive no benefits at all. Only 3% of low-income families receive assistance from six or more programs at once. Importantly, Medicaid and the school lunch program were the most common programs supporting these families, which would hopefully continue to exist in a post basic income world.

What Would People Do with a Basic Income?

Another significant hurdle to implementing a basic income is the assumption that large numbers of people would stop working and become "dependent" on the payment. When I asked 50 MTurk workers who were current or former public assistance recipients what they thought other people would do with $1000 monthly basic income, 46% believed that people would either quit working or work less, 16% thought people would apply the money toward major consumer purchases (vehicles, appliances, or electronics), and only 26% believed that people would continue working as they do now. In general, the respondents were skeptical that others would use the money well.

- "No one wants to work."
- "Because why would you need to work of you already have money? Duh."
- "I think this would make too many people lazy and would demotivate them to do better for themselves. I also think prices would skyrocket."
- "I think most people would buy more things they want."
- "I have noticed that people now a days will take everything they can get and then some like they are owed. I have known of a few different people that have worked the system to their own advantage and would boast about it."
- "Most people wouldn't work."
- "People like to buy things."
- "Most people aren't very fiscally responsible."
- "People love handouts, especially these days."
- "Most people would take the money and quit working and use the money for every day expenses."
- "It promotes negative laziness and does not promote acquiring an education or improving a way of life."
- "Many people would try to live within their means and not save for future problems."
- "Americans can be lazy so they'll do anything to reduce time at work."
- "I think most people would want to keep their regular income and just want to buy stuff with it."
- "Most people want to cut corners. Most people feel entitled to a break.…A lot of folks want something for nothing."

However, when I asked these same participants what *they* would do with a basic income, the responses were significantly different. Only two (4%) said they would quit working and another six (12%) said they would reduce their hours. Nearly half (42%) said they would continue working as they do now. As one respondent explained, "$1000 isn't anything these days, so I would keep working." Another elaborated that the UBI would help them transition to more fulfilling work: "I would use the money to live on and find something better to do with my time than some meaningless job." Allowing recipients the security and flexibility to move into personally meaningful work (perhaps in low paid human service positions or pursuing innovations in technology and art) is a primary advantage to a basic income scheme and has the potential to transform American civic and economic life. As one respondent explained, "I'd like the guaranteed income but still want to contribute to society."

A surprising 38% said that their priority would be to pursue major financial goals like purchasing a home, building emergency savings, starting a small business, going back to school, or paying down debt, compared to only one who said they would make a major consumer purchase.

- "I would use that money along with my current income to finance a house."
- "I'd use the money to go back to school for a graduate degree."
- "This amount would help me refocus my energies onto starting and expanding a business."
- "I would save the money until I was able to afford a home."
- "I would probably go back to school or start a computer repair business with some friends."
- "I would want to get a home in my name for my kids, then try to start up my own cleaning business in order to not need government assistance any longer."
- "I would use the $1000 per month to establish savings for the future."
- "I would use it to pay down debt."
- "I would continue working as I do now and any leftover money would go into a savings account for any future difficult times. I don't have health insurance so I like to have a fund for unexpected medical bills."
- "$1000 is more than I receive now and it would allow me to save any extra money in the hopes that someday I could afford a condo or start doing professional work again. The equipment I need would be expensive to buy out of pocket right now."
- "I would still try to live off of what I make online and use the $1000 as an investment either for a home or a business."
- "I would totally invest the money to save up for a house or maybe pay for private school for my kids!!"
- "I'd love to become debt free and feel like it was before I had acquired a bunch of debt that will follow me for what feels like

forever. Then I could look into starting my own business while working my current position with the $1000 per month."

- "I would utilize this basic income to improve my financial and medical situations by becoming a homeowner."
- "I would still work and save this money for my future and not touch it but save it."
- "I would apply the money toward home ownership and college for my children."
- "I would put it into a savings account for emergencies."
- "As it is now I am unable to keep anything in savings for major car repairs or unexpected home repairs so I would most likely try to put it away in a savings for unexpected emergencies or needs for my children."
- "Put it towards getting my masters."
- "I would keep working as I currently do but would reduce debt/increase savings."
- "I make less money than I need. I'm in school and working all the time, so I'd use it to pay for classes. I might also use it to invest in resources to set up passive income. I might also use it eventually toward a home down payment."
- "I would continue [working] as now and use that to pay off debt."
- "I would use the money and put it towards graduate school."

While it is difficult in survey research to separate what people say they would do from what they would *actually* do, these responses demonstrate two defining principles of the American welfare state, present since its inception: an industrious self-reliance and assumption of slothfulness in others. Politicians and their wealthy donors seeking to divert public funds to *their* priorities have been able to successfully exploit this division for hundreds of years, with only slight alterations to the rhetoric. Whether the perceived threat is a lack of religion, racial minorities, or unwed mothers, the message is the same: "they" are living it up on *your* hard-earned money. Savvy politicians know that those who are struggling to get by and could benefit from more equitable social policy are the most susceptible to this message.

But this framework can and has been overcome. The Alaska Permanent Fund, a distribution of oil profits to every adult resident since 1982, is overwhelmingly popular. A sample survey of Alaskan voters, 69% of whom are either Republican or Independent, found that 81% believe the fund improves their quality of life and 85% believe that it helps the state economy (Pew Research Center, 2014). Ninety percent believe that the program should continue to be universal. The fund is so popular that 64% of respondents would rather see an increase in their taxes than a repeal of the dividend (Isenberg, 2017). The Alaska fund may work because residents view oil resources as community property, with citizens entitled to a share of the profits. Whether it is funded from a natural resource such as oil or solar energy, or the prosperity created by our economic system, we will only realize a UBI when we can address the rhetoric of "us versus them." This debate is not between capitalism and socialism. The International Monetary Fund finds that reducing inequality is critical to sustained growth in modern economies (Berg & Ostry, 2011). In other words, the continued success of capitalism is entirely dependent on whether or not we can see all citizens as worthy of dignity and basic economic security.

If, as this book has explored, our historical and current models of support to low-income families are detrimental, both to the families themselves and to society at large, why do we continue on our current path? There seems to be widespread recognition that deep problems exist within the American welfare state and, increasingly, the proposed solution in the past 40 years has been to cut welfare budgets and tighten eligibility. The evidence is overwhelming that this approach has only exacerbated poverty and its societal consequences. Meanwhile, a growing body of literature presents us with a clear alternative. Trusting all people, including those with low-incomes, to make their own work, family, and financial decisions has a transformative impact on recipients and the communities around them. Those interested in eradicating poverty, dismantling a social safety net that primarily serves to punish the poor, and removing barriers to long-term financial stability are encouraged to contact their representatives in Congress and join advocacy groups such as the Basic Income Earth Network and the US Basic Income Guarantee.

References

Berg, A. G., & Ostry, J. D. (2011). *Inequality and Unsustainable Growth: Two Sides of the Same Coin?* (p. 21). Washington, DC: International Monetary Fund.

Center on Budget and Policy Priorities. (2018a). *Chart Book: SNAP Helps Struggling Families Put Food on the Table.* Retrieved from Center on Budget

Policies and Priorities Website: https://www.cbpp.org/research/food-assistance/chart-book-snap-helps-struggling-families-put-food-on-the-table

Center on Budget and Policy Priorities. (2018b). *Policy Basics: Supplemental Security Income*. Retrieved March 21, 2019, from Center on Budget and Policy Priorities Website: https://www.cbpp.org/research/social-security/policy-basics-supplemental-security-income

Center on Budget and Policy Priorities. (2018c). *Policy Basics: The Earned Income Tax Credit*. Retrieved from Center on Budget Policies and Priorities Website: https://www.cbpp.org/research/federal-tax/policy-basics-the-earned-income-tax-credit

Center on Budget and Policy Priorities. (2018d). *Policy Basics: The Supplemental Nutrition Assistance Program (SNAP)*. Retrieved from Center on Budget Policies and Priorities Website: https://www.cbpp.org/research/policy-basics-the-supplemental-nutrition-assistance-program-snap

Congressional Budget Office. (2013). *Refundable Tax Credits* (No. 4152). Retrieved from Congressional Budget Office Website: https://www.cbo.gov/publication/43767

Corasaniti, N. (2019, April 6). Booker Campaigns on Baby Bonds Program to Combat Inequality. *The New York Times*. Retrieved from https://www.nytimes.com/2019/04/06/us/politics/cory-booker-2020-baby-bonds.html

DeSilver, D. (2016). *The Biggest U.S. Tax Breaks*. Retrieved October 24, 2018, from Pew Research Center Website: http://www.pewresearch.org/fact-tank/2016/04/06/the-biggest-u-s-tax-breaks/

Edelstein, S., Pergamit, M., & Ratcliffe, C. (2014). *Characteristics of Families Receiving Multiple Public Benefits*. Washington, DC: Urban Institute.

Floyd, I., Pavetti, L., & Schott, L. (2015). *TANF Reaching Few Poor Families*. Retrieved from Center for Budget Policies and Priorities Website: https://www.cbpp.org/research/family-income-support/tanf-reaching-few-poor-families

Hoddinott, J., Gilligan, D., Hidrobo, M., Margolies, A., Roy, S., Sandström, S., et al. (n.d.). *Enhancing WFP's Capacity and Experience to Design, Implement, Monitor, and Evaluate Vouchers and Cash Transfer Programmes: Study Summary* (p. 15). Retrieved from International Food Policy Research Institute Website: http://ebrary.ifpri.org/utils/getfile/collection/p15738coll2/id/127961/filename/128172.pdf

Irving, S. K., & Loveless, T. A. (2015). *Dynamics of Economic Well-Being: Participation in Government Programs, 2009–2012: Who Gets Assistance?* Retrieved from U.S. Census Bureau Website: https://www.census.gov/content/dam/Census/library/publications/2015/demo/p70-141.pdf

Isenberg, T. J. (2017, June 28). *What a New Survey from Alaska Can Teach Us About Public Support for Basic Income*. Retrieved August 1, 2019, from Medium Website: https://medium.com/economicsecproj/what-a-new-survey-from-alaska-can-teach-us-about-public-support-for-basic-income-ccd0c3c16b42

Kasy, M. (2018). *Why a Universal Basic Income Is Better Than Subsidies of Low-Wage Work.* Retrieved from https://maxkasy.github.io/home/files/papers/UBI_EITC_Kasy.pdf

Marr, C., Huang, C.-C., Sherman, A., & Debot, B. (2015). *EITC and Child Tax Credit Promote Work, Reduce Poverty, and Support Children's Development, Research Finds.* Retrieved from Center on Budget Policies and Priorities Website: https://www.cbpp.org/research/federal-tax/eitc-and-child-tax-credit-promote-work-reduce-poverty-and-support-childrens

Nikiforos, M., Steinbaum, M., & Zezza, G. (2017). *Modeling the Macroeconomic Effects of a Universal Basic Income.* Retrieved from Roosevelt Institute Website: http://rooseveltinstitute.org/modeling-macroeconomic-effects-ubi/

Pew Research Center. (2014). *Party Affiliation by State—Religion in America: U.S. Religious Data, Demographics and Statistics | Pew Research Center.* Retrieved August 1, 2019, from Religion and Public Life Website: https://www.pewforum.org/religious-landscape-study/

Piper, K. (2018, October 16). *Early Childhood Education Yields Big Benefits—Just Not the Ones You Think.* Retrieved July 27, 2019, from Vox Website: https://www.vox.com/future-perfect/2018/10/16/17928164/early-childhood-education-doesnt-teach-kids-fund-it

Piper, K. (2019, January 8). *Study: Head Start Improves Kids' Lives. But We're Still Finding Out Just How.* Retrieved July 27, 2019, from Vox Website: https://www.vox.com/future-perfect/2019/1/8/18166068/study-head-start-child-poverty

Quinnipiac University. (2019, July 29). *QU Poll Release Detail.* Retrieved July 30, 2019, from QU Poll Website: https://poll.qu.edu/national/release-detail?ReleaseID=3635

Rice, F. (2019, May 22). *Cryptocurrencies: GoodDollar—The First Blockchain-Related UBI Conference Talk.* Retrieved from https://basicincome.org/news/2019/05/cryptocurrencies-gooddollar-the-first-blockchain-related-ubi-conference-talk/

Rodrigo, C. M. (2019, July 29). *Yang Qualifies for Third and Fourth Democratic Debates [Text].* Retrieved July 30, 2019, from The Hill Website: https://thehill.com/homenews/campaign/455207-yang-qualifies-for-third-and-fourth-democratic-debates

Stayton, R. (2019). *Solar Dividends: How Solar Energy Can Generate a Basic Income for Everyone on Earth.* Inverness, Scotland: Sandstone Publishing.

Stein, J. (2019, June 6). Rep. Rashida Tlaib Introduces Closest Plan in Congress to Universal Basic Income. *Washington Post.* Retrieved from https://www.washingtonpost.com/us-policy/2019/06/06/rep-rashida-tlaib-introduces-closest-plan-congress-universal-basic-income/

Tanner, M., & Hughes, C. (2013). *The Work Versus Welfare Trade-Off: 2013 An Analysis of the Total Level of Welfare Benefits by State.* Washington, DC: Cato Institute.

The Earned Income Tax Credit Almost Pays for Itself. (2018, November 24). *The Economist.* Retrieved from https://www.economist.com/united-states/2018/11/24/the-earned-income-tax-credit-almost-pays-for-itself
US Department of Health and Human Services. (2019, February 1). *Poverty Guidelines.* Retrieved May 1, 2019, from ASPE Website: https://aspe.hhs.gov/poverty-guidelines
Whitehurst, G. J. (2001). *Family Support or School Readiness? Contrasting Models of Public Spending on Children's Early Care and Learning.* Retrieved from Brookings Institution Website: https://www.brookings.edu/research/family-support-or-school-readiness-contrasting-models-of-public-spending-on-childrens-early-care-and-learning/
Widerquist, K. (2017). The Cost of Basic Income: Back-of-the-Envelope Calculations. *Basic Income Studies, 12*(2). https://doi.org/10.1515/bis-2017-0016.
Wiederspan, J., Rhodes, E., & Shaefer, H. L. (2015). Expanding the Discourse on Antipoverty Policy: Reconsidering a Negative Income Tax. *Journal of Poverty, 19*(2), 218–238. https://doi.org/10.1080/10875549.2014.991889.
Wright, S. (2018, October 18). *Senator Harris Proposes Bold Tax Breaks for the Middle Class.* Retrieved October 29, 2018, from Ebony Website: https://www.ebony.com/news/senator-harris-proposes-bold-tax-breaks-for-the-middle-class/
Yee Hee Lee, M. (2014a, December 5). Do 'Welfare' Recipients Get $35,000 in Benefits a Year? *The Washington Post.* Retrieved from https://www.washingtonpost.com/news/fact-checker/wp/2014/12/05/grothman-single-parents-welfare/?utm_term=.cb1f52f555d4

Index

L. Hamilton, *Welfare Doesn't Work*, Exploring the Basic Income Guarantee, https://doi.org/10.1007/978-3-030-37121-0